CORRUPTION: A DANGER TO DEMOCRACY IN EUROPE AND EURASIA

HEARING

BEFORE THE

SUBCOMMITTEE ON EUROPE, EURASIA, AND EMERGING THREATS

OF THE

COMMITTEE ON FOREIGN AFFAIRS
HOUSE OF REPRESENTATIVES

ONE HUNDRED FOURTEENTH CONGRESS

SECOND SESSION

_____

DECEMBER 7, 2016

_____

Serial No. 114–240

_____

Printed for the use of the Committee on Foreign Affairs

Available via the World Wide Web: http://www.foreignaffairs.house.gov/ or http://www.gpo.gov/fdsys/

_____

U.S. GOVERNMENT PUBLISHING OFFICE

22–866PDF   WASHINGTON : 2017

COMMITTEE ON FOREIGN AFFAIRS

EDWARD R. ROYCE, California, *Chairman*

CHRISTOPHER H. SMITH, New Jersey
ILEANA ROS-LEHTINEN, Florida
DANA ROHRABACHER, California
STEVE CHABOT, Ohio
JOE WILSON, South Carolina
MICHAEL T. McCAUL, Texas
TED POE, Texas
MATT SALMON, Arizona
DARRELL E. ISSA, California
TOM MARINO, Pennsylvania
JEFF DUNCAN, South Carolina
MO BROOKS, Alabama
PAUL COOK, California
RANDY K. WEBER SR., Texas
SCOTT PERRY, Pennsylvania
RON DeSANTIS, Florida
MARK MEADOWS, North Carolina
TED S. YOHO, Florida
CURT CLAWSON, Florida
SCOTT DesJARLAIS, Tennessee
REID J. RIBBLE, Wisconsin
DAVID A. TROTT, Michigan
LEE M. ZELDIN, New York
DANIEL DONOVAN, New York

ELIOT L. ENGEL, New York
BRAD SHERMAN, California
GREGORY W. MEEKS, New York
ALBIO SIRES, New Jersey
GERALD E. CONNOLLY, Virginia
THEODORE E. DEUTCH, Florida
BRIAN HIGGINS, New York
KAREN BASS, California
WILLIAM KEATING, Massachusetts
DAVID CICILLINE, Rhode Island
ALAN GRAYSON, Florida
AMI BERA, California
ALAN S. LOWENTHAL, California
GRACE MENG, New York
LOIS FRANKEL, Florida
TULSI GABBARD, Hawaii
JOAQUIN CASTRO, Texas
ROBIN L. KELLY, Illinois
BRENDAN F. BOYLE, Pennsylvania

AMY PORTER, *Chief of Staff*   THOMAS SHEEHY, *Staff Director*
JASON STEINBAUM, *Democratic Staff Director*

————

SUBCOMMITTEE ON EUROPE, EURASIA, AND EMERGING THREATS

DANA ROHRABACHER, California, *Chairman*

TED POE, Texas
TOM MARINO, Pennsylvania
MO BROOKS, Alabama
PAUL COOK, California
RANDY K. WEBER SR., Texas
REID J. RIBBLE, Wisconsin
DAVID A. TROTT, Michigan

GREGORY W. MEEKS, New York
ALBIO SIRES, New Jersey
THEODORE E. DEUTCH, Florida
WILLIAM KEATING, Massachusetts
LOIS FRANKEL, Florida
TULSI GABBARD, Hawaii

CONTENTS

CORRUPTION: A DANGER TO DEMOCRACY IN EUROPE AND EURASIA

WEDNESDAY, DECEMBER 7, 2016

House of Representatives,
Subcommittee on Europe, Eurasia, and Emerging Threats,
Committee on Foreign Affairs,
Washington, DC.

The subcommittee met, pursuant to notice, at 10:05 a.m., in room 2172, Rayburn House Office Building, Hon. Dana Rohrabacher (chairman of the subcommittee) presiding.

Mr. ROHRABACHER. I hereby call this hearing of the Europe, Eurasia, and Emerging Threats Subcommittee into order. This will be the final subcommittee event of the year, and I must say it has been a pleasure to chair this subcommittee and to serve with my friend and colleague and ranking member, Mr. Meeks.

Mr. Meeks, thank you so much. We have had a good 2 years together here. We will see what happens next time around. No one knows. I very much look forward to continued collaboration one way or the other in the new Congress.

So with that said, for this hearing we are focusing on corruption in Europe and Eurasia. This issue has not been really the recipient of much attention. It certainly hasn't received the attention it deserves. Both globally and in particular countries this committee oversees it seems that this issue just hasn't really been touched on. It is like maybe some sort of a hot stove.

But the corruption, we have to recognize, has been a major factor since the end of the cold war in the former Soviet states. These countries have worked with various degrees of success to privatize their own state-owned industries and build various institutions that allow for democracy and prosperity.

In short, for them corruption has been a common stumbling block to progress, as it is also, as we recognize, in Third World countries, whether or not it is petty corruption, perhaps by a police officer who is looking to give you a ticket or, at a grander level of corruption, where private interests actually capture control of large chunks of state assets. It hampers reforms, corruption holds back economic growth, and in far too many cases it also impoverishes low-income populations in countries that could be doing much better for their entire population.

Now, when government institutions serve private interests, enriching oligarchs and enriching politicians instead of addressing the needs of its people, that undermines the faith in government and the rule of law, it undermines the basic stability and any chance

(1)

for prosperity, at least any chance for ordinary people to live in prosperity in these countries.

Hence, if we understand the general aim of U.S. policy as promoting prosperous, peaceful, and pluralistic countries, fighting corruption should be at the center of that effort. Unfortunately, it is not, and perhaps because there are powerful Western accomplices to these crimes of corruption in developing countries.

While we should call out and hold accountable corrupt officials, it is important to understand that in some places corruption is the rule, not the exception. I would like to cite a recent survey released by Transparency International that found that one in three people living in Europe and Central Asia believe corruption to be one of the largest problems of their country.

Policymakers in the United States and Europe need to think about broad and systematic approaches to this challenge. For example, Western banks, are they complicit in money laundering for corrupt officials? Does that make them an accomplice to the theft of resources that should serve the poorest and most vulnerable people of the world, but instead those resources are being utilized and the profit from it are going to large financial institutions in cooperation with local gangsters and thugs in those countries?

What about us? Could we do more to ensure that corrupt officials can't store their ill-gotten gains in Western banks or use it to buy property or businesses in our country?

This is too much for today, it is too much for just today, but it will be the subject for an investigative hearing or investigative hearings in the years ahead, whether I am here or not.

I am looking forward to a discussion today of these things with our witnesses, and I look forward to their testimonies. And without objection, their written statements will be made part of the record.

And I will turn to my ranking member, Mr. Gregory Meeks.

Mr. MEEKS. I want to thank you, Mr. Chairman, for calling this timely hearing—our last. I guess, this will be our last of the 114th Congress——

Mr. ROHRABACHER. That is why it was timely.

Mr. MEEKS [continuing]. To discuss the role of corruption and eroding democracy in Europe. And I do appreciate your cooperation in working together over the last couple—last 4 years actually—and to work more on Europe together. My intentions are to stay here, you know, we will be in the next Congress—unless you, of course, have other plans.

Mr. ROHRABACHER. We will see. Don't count on it.

Mr. MEEKS. So hopefully we will do this again.

The fight against corruption is a civic duty, and I am against corruption here in the United States just as much as I am against corruption in Ukraine, France, and Russia, or anywhere on the planet. I think we can all agree on that. And corruption is often ill-defined, ambiguous, and sometimes woven in with cultural norms.

Yet, while it take many forms, we know that it has costs. When bad actors in the public sector use political power to enrich themselves, there are consequences. The state is less effective and citizens less trusting of its political leaders.

They do not act alone. Government officials who steal public money often use legal loopholes to launder their loot abroad in real estate or offshore accounts. This is done by employing willing enablers, lawyers or business partners, who take the money while looking the other way.

Now, I have found it important when speaking of corruption in Europe that I can't avoid mentioning particularly the role of the Russian Government and Russia itself in exporting corruption abroad. The Russian Government has successfully muddied the waters in the media and politics with its dirty money in neighboring countries looking to reform, notably Ukraine, Moldova, and Montenegro. This is very troubling.

Furthermore, the Russian taxpayer rubles have found sanctuary here in the United States and across Europe, giving us more reason for concern. And while Ukraine struggles to reform and create ambitious, transparent systems for the benefit of its people, we see Russian businesses and politicians with significant influence in trying to make us think that Ukraine can never reform.

It is not only a morally troubling situation, it is also a national security question. It is one thing to look away when another country's government robs its own people; it is another to allow that government to use its citizens' money to corrupt and meddle in our democratic, rule-of-law-based society.

This is the one reason I will continue to demand—I will continue to demand—here in the United States that President-elect Trump release his tax returns and completely divest from his international companies. The American people have a right to know who our President may be beholden to.

Now, fortunately for some of us, there are brave investigative journalists, lawyers, and activists who have shed light on the kleptocracy in the Kremlin and the way the Russian people are worse off because of it. Because Russia did not successfully reform after the fall of the Soviet Union and yet is home to vast amounts of natural resources, it is ripe territory for corruption at the highest levels.

One of those brave men is here with us today. And I want to thank Mr. Kolesnikov for your bravery and work for the Russian people. I look forward to hearing your testimony and your firsthand knowledge of what drives the highest levels of Russian Government.

I want to let you know that there is a reason why we should focus on Russia here today. It is because we believe that Russia is an important country, a potential partner. Russia can be better, can reform, and can be democratic and can be free.

As a senior member of the Financial Services Committee, I am also deeply interested in how we can safeguard our financial institutions from corruption. It is that vulnerability to foreign and malign influences that worries me. What laws should we consider to amend beneficial ownership, for example? What are the risks today to American sovereignty in these areas?

So, again, I want to thank you and all of our witnesses. And I look forward to working with my colleagues and to keep America and our allies safe from the unvirtuous spiral of corruption. And I yield back.

Mr. ROHRABACHER. We have been joined by two of our other colleagues. Do either of our other colleagues have an opening statement?

Mr. Connolly, you are welcome to. You are not on the committee, but you are welcome to have an opening statement.

Mr. CONNOLLY. Thank you, Mr. Chairman.

And I want to associate myself with the remarks just made by my good friend from New York. And I also salute the bravery of our guest witness here today. Thank you for participating.

And I would ask unanimous consent my full statement be entered into the record at this time.

Mr. ROHRABACHER. Without objection.

Mr. CONNOLLY. I thank the chair, and I thank my good friend Mr. Meeks.

Mr. ROHRABACHER. And Mr. Weber has decided not to have an opening statement; although, I am sure he would like to comment on how the Democratic candidates deserve to be investigated in our last election in their financial dealings as well. But I won't put words into his mouth, but I thought somebody needed to make that point.

So with that said, I would like to welcome the witnesses. And if we could, if you could summarize your testimony in 5-minute segments, and then we will get into the questions and answers. And what I will do is I will introduce all of you and then we will start with Mr. Davidson after this introduction.

So we have Charles Davidson, who is the executive director of Kleptocracy Initiative at the Hudson Institute, as well as being the publisher of the American Interest magazine. The Kleptocracy Initiative and its stated goal is to conduct original research into the growing threat posed by democracies by autocratic regimes structured as kleptocracies.

And I think it will be very fascinating to get into some definitions, not only kleptocracy but exactly what is corruption and what is not corruption. And looking forward to your testimony.

And then we have also with us Ivan Vejvoda, who is a senior vice president for programs at the German Marshall Fund here in Washington. From 2010 to 2013 he was the executive director of that organization's Balkan Trust for Democracy Program. Before that, he was an adviser to the Serbian Government and a long-time advocate of democracy in that region and honest government.

And we have also with us today, and as we heard from Mr. Meeks, a Russian-born businessman, Mr. Sergei Kolesnikov.

Is that right? Did I get it?

Mr. KOLESNIKOV. Kolesnikov.

Mr. ROHRABACHER. Okay. And we are very happy to have you with us today.

He is a Russian-born businessman who has traveled from outside the United States to come here today to testify at this hearing. In 2010, he left Russia and went to the press about certain allegations of high-level corruption within the Russian Government.

So today we are going to be focusing on corruption both in theory and definitions of what is and what is taking place, but also in specifics in terms of different examples of corruption that are going on and how they impact—which is important—how that corruption impacts the people of the countries which are suffering from that corruption of their government.

So with that said, Mr. Davidson, you may begin your 5-minute presentation.

STATEMENT OF MR. CHARLES DAVIDSON, EXECUTIVE DIRECTOR, KLEPTOCRACY INITIATIVE, HUDSON INSTITUTE

Mr. DAVIDSON. Mr. Chairman, Ranking Member Meeks, and distinguished members of the subcommittee, I appreciate the invitation to appear before you today. And I must say, these opening statements were so impressive to me. I think that Chairman Rohrabacher's statement perfectly summarizes the overall issue. And I agree with everything that Mr. Meeks said.

So I will try to run through my statement very rapidly and touch on this enabler issue which was brought up, and go to the conclusions as to what we can do about this sort of thing. So I am going to gloss over agreeing with you on these various matters.

And in terms of what corruption does to societies in undermining rule of law, subverting institutions, encouraging cultures of lawlessness, how it impoverishes the citizens of these countries, we all see this. I think it is worth reminding ourselves again and again that the Maidan Revolution was really about corruption. All those young people were talking about corruption all the time. It was really the driver of that revolution.

And in terms of the definitions and how all this evolved, institutionalized corruption, when it becomes the norm and consolidates its political power and we get actual state capture, that is what we talk about at least in terms of being kleptocracy. It is when corruption has really taken over the state and we get the rule of thieves.

And obviously, these kleptocratic regimes have little appetite for democracy. I think an important point, in particular for our business community, is that these regimes have very little taste for free-market competition, so little taste that, in fact, corruption and exporting it is sort of an existential issue for them. They can't compete in the free market.

And we have, indeed, as was mentioned, been a partner in this whole system. And the way that has worked—and we published an article about this called, ''Stage Hands: How Western Enablers Facilitate Kleptocracy''—well, first, you have got to be able to loot the country, take it out of the country and put it in a safe place. We provide that safe place. Then, of course, there is a third stage where you hire public relations people and you put your children in the right schools and you become a full-fledged member of the West and become a very respectable person.

And I think another thing we need to focus on more is the issue of incentive. When we do this, when we provide this safe haven, we are incentivizing corruption, and then we are further incentivizing all the way to kleptocracy. And this is something we really need to think about, and stop providing the punch bowl, if you will.

The Ukrainian example we have already looked at.

We don't really talk enough about authoritarianism in all of this. What we see now with the authoritarian threats is that authoritarian regimes that have become very militarily aggressive—and there are two I have in mind, which I barely need to name. They both happen to be structured as kleptocracies. Their elites are keeping their loot in the West, in our banks and financial institutions, in our real estate. And you would think we have a little bit of leverage over them, perhaps more than we are using.

On this overall issue I mentioned, we published a paper called ''The Kleptocracy Curse,'' which may be of interest, which is almost an expansion of Chairman Rohrabacher's initial statement, expands on all those points.

What can we do? I have 33 seconds to talk about that, and I will go right to the issue of anonymous companies, shell companies, whatever we want to call them. There are a few other recommendations in the testimony, they all pale in the face of the importance of the anonymous company question, in my opinion and in the opinion of many people that I have spoken with in law enforcement and the State Department, private investigators, large private investigator firms. There seems to be a real consensus that this is a huge part of the problem.

And I will leave it at that. Thank you very much.

[The prepared statement of Mr. Davidson follows:]

STATEMENT OF CHARLES DAVIDSON
Executive Director, Kleptocracy Initiative, Hudson Institute
Corruption: A Danger to Democracy in Europe and Eurasia
Subcommittee on Europe, Eurasia, and Emerging Threats
U.S. House of Representatives
December 7, 2016

Chairman Rohrabacher, Ranking Member Meeks, and distinguished members of the Subcommittee, I appreciate the invitation to appear before you today.

Corruption: A Danger to Democracy in Europe and Eurasia

Institutionalized corruption in Europe and Eurasia remains an ongoing challenge to U.S. efforts to promote stable, prosperous, and democratic countries. Corruption undermines rule of law, prevents or subverts institutions from functioning honestly, and encourages cultures of lawlessness. It is generally accepted that the distress that led to the Maidan revolution in Ukraine was primarily a revolt against corruption, and we struggle in our efforts to promote a democratic and free ally there.

When "institutionalized corruption" becomes the norm, and consolidates its political power, when there is "state capture," we find ourselves facing "kleptocracies," nations "ruled by thieves." These kleptocratic regimes have no appetite for democracy. And they can't withstand free market competition, so corruption of their partners is an existential issue for them.

Across Eurasia, Western diplomats are increasingly ignored when they warn of corruption. Indeed, Western anti-corruption talk is increasingly taken as hypocrisy despite decades of diplomatic effort to support more democratic and transparent societies in Eurasia.[1] How have we reached this state of affairs?

The West has been a Partner in the Plunder of Eurasian States

When a corrupt official or kleptocrat seeks to secure his or her illicitly gained assets, they seek a safe haven, with rule of law protecting property rights. The West, generally speaking, has provided this haven. We have published a paper that describes this process in detail, *Stage Hands: How Western Enablers Facilitate Kleptocracy.*[2]

Providing a safe haven for the proceeds of corruption establishes an incentive for corrupt practices. In my view this question of incentivization has been neglected, and is key to understanding the overall political challenge faced in terms of reform.

Let us take a Ukrainian example. Under the Yanukovych regime it has been alleged that billions of dollars were stolen at the expense of the state. This theft impoverished already rudimentary public services, delegitimized the regime, and ultimately contributed to its downfall (the Maidan in the first instance a revolt against

---

[1] Ben Judah, *How Offshore Finance Sank Western Soft Power*, Kleptocracy Initiative, Hudson Institute, March 2015. http://kleptocracyinitiative.org/2015/03/how-offshore-finance-sank-western-soft-power/
[2] Oliver Bullough, *Stage Hands: How Western Enablers Facilitate Kleptocracy*, Kleptocracy Initiative, Hudson Institute, May 2016. http://www.hudson.org/research/12463-stage-hands

corruption). A significant portion of this money left the country and entered Western jurisdictions.

Kleptocracy Wrecks Eurasian Democratization

The role of the Western financial system is a major reason why democracies failed to take root in all but a few states in Eurasia following the collapse of the USSR. A golden age of money laundering incentivized state plunder for post-Soviet Eurasian elites. By way of illustration, Russia allegedly lost at least $211.5 billion in illicit financial outflows from 1994 to 2011,[3] whilst since 2004 Ukraine has lost over $116 billion.[4]

Plundered wealth could be laundered and safeguarded, and converted into well-funded new sources of power. This helped steer what was hoped to be a transition to democracy towards a new kleptocratic authoritarian political model.

In our most recent paper we call this *The Kleptocracy Curse*, which describes among other things the role of Western enablers regarding institutionalized corruption in Eurasia.[5] This is starkly visible in Ukraine, which failed to build either a market economy or a functioning state, fuelling revolutionary discontent. As Western diplomats struggled to impress on Kyiv's politicians the value of the rule of law, Ukrainian elites were stashing wealth in the West. This happens across Eurasia, where authoritarian elites now treat London, New York, and other Western jurisdictions as corruption services centers.

What are the Costs?

Ignoring the kleptocracy curse risks further political damage. Democratic development and free markets are undermined. Regimes hostile to our values expand their power and influence.

The current state of Europe offers a warning. The Parliamentary Assembly of the Council of Europe, the continent's oldest human rights institution, has been corrupted and silenced by an authoritarian kleptocratic regime. In France, the leading populist opposition is financed in part by a non-democratic autocracy. Members of the British establishment have business ties to elites from arguably non-democratic, autocratic kleptocracies, even forming an emerging lobby.

The idea of the West as a community of values is critically threatened.

---

[3] Dev Karr and Sarah Freitas, *Russia: Illicit Financial Flows and the Role of the Underground Economy*, Global Financial Integrity, February 2013. http://www.gfintegrity.org/press-release/russia-hemorrhages-least-us211-5-billion-illicit-financial-outflows-1994-2011-new-gfi-study/
[4] Dev Karr and Joseph Spanjers, *Illicit Financial Flows From Developing Countries: 2004-2013*, Global Financial Integrity, December 2015. http://www.gfintegrity.org/report/illicit-financial-flows-from-developing-countries-2004-2013/
[5] Ben Judah, *The Kleptocracy Curse: Rethinking Containment*, Kleptocracy Initiative, Hudson Institute, November 2016. http://www.hudson.org/research/12928-the-kleptocracy-curse-rethinking-containment

What is to be done?

In terms of what we can do, there is one step that in my view is indispensible, and that is doing away with anonymous shell companies, setting an example that can be leveraged to persuade our allies to follow suit. This notion has been underscored by discussions with law enforcement, private investigators, lawyers, international finance experts and others. Anonymous shell companies are the prime vehicle for concealing ownership of assets and safeguarding the proceeds of corruption, and are used regarding both financial assets and real estate.[6]

A second priority should be seeking other ways to curtail our enabling role, blocking and tackling the nooks and crannies of international finance that are conduits for corrupt proceeds.

We also need to empower our law enforcement to tackle egregious cases, and look into amending the Foreign Corrupt Practices Act to include penalizing the bribe takers.

In parallel we should be vigilant regarding the influence of foreign institutionalized corruption on US soil, for example strengthening the Foreign Agents Registration Act and its enforcement, and strengthening interdictions and monitoring of those representing regimes where institutionalized corruption is a way of life.

---

[6] Nate Sibley, *Kleptocracy, Inc.: How America Enables Global Corruption*, Kleptocracy Initiative, Hudson Institute, October 2016. http://www.hudson.org/research/12911-kleptocracy-inc-how-america-enables-global-corruption

Mr. ROHRABACHER. You may proceed.

STATEMENT OF MR. IVAN VEJVODA, SENIOR VICE PRESIDENT FOR PROGRAMS, THE GERMAN MARSHALL FUND OF THE UNITED STATES

Mr. VEJVODA. Mr. Chairman, Ranking Member, members of the committee, thank you very much for the invitation to testify before you today on this important subject, as we have heard both from the introductory statements and from my colleague Charles Davidson.

Democratic transitions after 1989 confront the issue of the fact that there was practically no democratic political culture in the post-Communist space, in the space where one party ruled there was no pluralism, and where human rights were unknown to peo- ple. And so it had to begin with, as Hannah Arendt would put it, giving people the right, to understand that they have a right to have rights.

And so the legacy of the old, the inertia of the old corrupt ways lives on as the democratic transition advances and as the democratic political culture tries to find its roots. And probably the best comparison is between Poland and Ukraine that had the same level of economic development in 1990. We see where Poland is today and we see what has happened to Ukraine, complete differences in standards of living and the institutional democratic culture, not that Poland is without problems today, as we know.

The political winners of the Communist system—the political losers as democratic transition happens become the economic winners because they have all the inside information. They have the network through the secret services. And ultimately, as economic winners, they again become the political winners because of the nexus between the oligarchic structures and political parties.

One particularly difficult issue that is addressed is that of political parties themselves, as they rise from nowhere after the crumbling of the Communist system. And the problem there is the financing of political parties. Where do these parties find moneys to actually have a party structure throughout a country?

And that means, of course, that they have to lean on private business, and this is where a lot of the corrupt practices between the politics and economics, to speak all too gently, happens and where a lot of the corrupt practices. Of course, in Western societies we know that there are also these kinds of issues, but I would really like to highlight that problem in addressing the issue of corruption.

I, unfortunately, coming from the former Yugoslavia and Serbia, had to live through the worst of a criminalization of society and the state of Serbia under sanctions that were imposed in 1992. For a country under sanctions to survive, it goes into full corrupt mode.

And so when we emerged from the Milosevic regime in 2000, this was the state of affairs that we had to confront, how does one start pushing back this criminalization that was pervasive through the state. And of course it requires what other post-Communist countries do, and that is to reinforce the structures of democratic institutions, of structural reform, et cetera.

But that, as you know, requires support from the outside. And the role that the United States, Canada, the European Union member states, with their support through USAID, through development agencies has been extremely important.

It, of course, behooves the citizens and governments in each of these countries, whether we are talking about Ukraine, Moldova, Serbia, Montenegro, Albania, Kosovo, to actually do the work of reform. They need to be the stakeholders. They need to sense the desire of citizens to have a society democratic based on the rule of law and human rights.

And so that burden is principally on them, but it cannot be done without the principle of solidarity that we have seen delivered through these 25 and more years. And it requires in terms of what is to be done a holistic approach, and some of it we have already heard from Charles Davidson. So support to journalists, investigative reporting, support to civil society that pressures from below the governments to make them more accountable and responsible. Customs are an extremely sensitive point.

But the key and the backbone is judicial reform, a truly independent judiciary where citizens feel that no one is above the law and that everyone gets a fair trial. And we see the difficulties in acquiring fully independent judiciaries.

And so I would urge that the continuing work of USAID with the European Union in support of these democratic processes is one of the backbones, as I said, along with the citizens themselves and their elected officials pushing toward strengthening the rule of law and creating further stability for democratic political culture.

[The prepared statement of Mr. Vejvoda follows:]

United States Congress

House of Representatives

Committee on Foreign Affairs

Subcommittee on Europe, Eurasia and Emerging Threats

Hearing:

CORRUPTION: A DANGER TO DEMOCRACY IN EUROPE AND EURASIA

December 7, 2016

Washington D.C.

TESTIMONY

IVAN VEJVODA

Senior Vice President / Programs

The German Marshall Fund of the United States

Mr. Chairman, thank you for the invitation to come and testify before you today. It is an honor to be here before this Subcommittee of the House of Representatives of the U.S. Congress. I am here to offer my personal views on the current issues regarding corruption as well as to assess the progress made in combatting this scourge.

Introduction:

The Oxford dictionary defines corruption as "the perversion or destruction of integrity in the discharge of public duties by bribery and favor".

No country in the world is immune at some level from such bad practices. There are different degrees of corruption from small scale, petty, through bigger all the way to systemic corruption capturing a whole state and society.

The main bulwark to broader, encompassing forms of corruption is democracy. Functioning democratic institutions based on the rule of law within a framework of division of powers between the legislative, executive and judiciary, are key to upholding public integrity, responsible and accountable governance and curtailing the pursuit of all forms of favoritism, nepotism, clientelism, bribery, embezzlement, fraud in short of abuse of public office, but also abuse in the private sector..

Liberal democratic societies based on the rule of law have known egregious examples of corruption, but in the majority of cases these have been uncovered and prosecuted, thanks to the existence of norms, laws, rules and regulations that are successfully implemented and enforced.

It is important to note that there is also a significant international, cross-border dimension to corruption in the form of tax evasion through off-shore sites. The latest example of this was revealed in the so-called Panama Papers. Money laundering through a variety of mechanisms and laws that allow the easy registration, setting of "tax-friendly" companies, is often ubiquitous in some countries. Those holding money, cash, acquired through corrupt, fraudulent practices will try and hide it and or "launder" it so as to then inject into legal activities.

Banking secrecy, shielding people who avoid tax payments in their own countries, has been addressed more vigorously in recent years. For example, Switzerland over the past years has made agreements to share information on those holding assets in its banks. Switzerland's banks housed around $2.1 trillion, or 27%, of offshore wealth, according to the Boston Consulting Group in 2012.

International auditing firms have a great responsibility as well given that they are present in all countries and can be the ones who can expose fraudulent activities and assess the business environment and serve as warning mechanisms to potential investors but also thus serve the public good.

All of these dimensions need to be taken into consideration when diagnosing the causes of the disease of corruption affecting the polity and body politic of the countries of the post-communist space and ways to combat it. The correct diagnosis of the ill is crucial for finding the impactful remedies to combat this blight.

Tracking corruption and proposing remedies

At international and domestic levels there are a number of initiatives that help follow the levels of corruption in any given state. The *United Nations Convention against Corruption* (UNCAC) was signed in 2003. This was the first legally binding international anti-corruption instrument. International financial institutions such as the *International Monetary Fund* and the *World Bank*, the *European Bank for Reconstruction and Development*, *European Investment Bank*, to name a few, have a variety of tools and instruments by which they gauge for example the state capture compared to state autonomy, and who through their support and investment mechanisms condition and enforce good governance practices.

Transparency International one of the prime organizations tracking levels of corruptions publishes an annual Corruption Perceptions Index since 1995.

The chair of Transparency International José Ugaz, has said: Countries at the bottom [of the Corruption Perception Index] need to adopt radical anti-corruption measures in favor of their people. Countries at the top of the index should make sure they don't export corrupt practices to underdeveloped countries." There are always lurking temptations in major companies, multilateral or other from established democracies to seek "short-cuts", through bribes and otherwise to acquire contracts in developing countries – the responsibility to fight corruption is paramount at every level and in all quarters. That is why for example the United States' Foreign Corrupt Practices Act of 1977 was a harbinger of ways to address the issue of corruption from the standpoint of developed nations.

The *United Nations Development Program's* 16 Sustainable Development Goals offer a combination of activities that create conditions in a polity for strengthening democratic institutions and bettering the socio-economic environment, which can lead to diminishing corruption

An important initiative the *European Research Center for Anti-Corruption and State-Building* based in Berlin has made important contributions to among other "develop a second generation of governance indicators to allow better monitoring of anti-corruption trends (time-sensitive) and the impact of policies (change-sensitive)", but equally importantly takes a necessary holistic approach as to how to confront and combat corruption.

The *Kleptocracy Initiative* is another excellent example of tracking and informing the public of corrupt practices worldwide.

Eastern Europe, South Eastern Europe and the Black Sea Region:

Prologue: the old regime and the revolution

Corruption is a major threat to democracy as it undermines democratic institutions and their credibility.

States and societies that were communist until the fall of the Berlin wall or shortly thereafter have undergone or are in various phases of democratic transition, democratic consolidation or, regretfully of democratic regression, in which democratic institutions are frail and where implementation of existing, even sometimes exemplary anti-corruption laws, is lacking. Corruption takes on forms that can and often do lead to state capture by oligarchic groups linked to political parties and factions.

Many are the reasons for this. It was clear from the outset, after 1989, if not for all, that democratic take a long time and that they do not follow a unilinear path. The shining façade of democracy does not appear suddenly or automatically as the old façade of totalitarianism or authoritarianism crumbles. Alexis de Tocqueville in his seminal work The Old Regime and the Revolution two centuries ago underscored how the old authoritarian habits and views live on as a society tries to change, and often are able to rear their ugly head. Ralf Dahrendorf in his book published in 1990 *Reflections on the Revolution Europe* wrote: it takes six months to create new political institutions; to write a constitution and electoral laws. "It takes six months to create new political institutions; to write a constitution and electoral laws. It may take six years to create a half-viable economy. It will probably take 60 years to create a civil society". Maybe this is an exaggeration but it emphasizes that creating the norms and behaviors of a democratic institutional culture require time. This is of course not an excuse or justification for the hard work of change and struggle to consolidate democratic institutions and the rule of law.

It is important to underscore that the task is one that foremost behooves the citizens and elected officials of the countries in question. They are the ones who bear the burden of responsibility to create within their society more equitable conditions, laws and democratic institutions leading to stability, peace and prosperity. But in the spirit of the modern principle of solidarity it is also important that support is given to those who are in need and striving to better their condition.

In the case of the countries in question the transatlantic alliance, the United States, Canada and the European Union have in these past 25 years, continue and in future should continue to support these countries overcome their legacies of the past, their old regimes. Especially knowing that there are no immediate, quick-fixes, but that these are mid to long-term processes.

Key to the success is judicial reform and the creation of an independent judiciary. This is the backbone of the rule of law in a democracy and the institution by which citizens feel the fairness of the system through the dispensation of justice, due process where everyone gets a fair trial and where no one is above or outside of the reach of law.

Corruption and ways to stifle and overcome it in Eastern Europe: The Black Sea Region

Each country is a story unto itself.

The entry of Romania and Bulgaria into the European Union in 2007 and the "big bang enlargement" of the EU in 2004, was, and still is criticized as a premature step, the reasoning being that they were not sufficiently reformed, and not further along the path of strengthening their democratic institutions, with still significant levels of corruption. This may be the case, but it is important to raise this case as an example of the historical and geopolitical importance of the decision to incorporate these two countries even though they effectively were not up to par with the countries that entered in 2004 (Czech Republic, Estonia, Hungary, Latvia, Lithuania, Poland, Slovakia, Slovenia and Cyprus and Malta).

They have in the meantime during these 9 years made significant advances, Romania in particular. Romania developed a successful anti-corruption institution that showed the way forward not only for the region but for many other countries. As is always the case, leadership, even statesmanship is essential in moving things forward. A very important role was played by Minister of Justice Monica Macovei (2004-2007). She courageously spearheaded an effort to move against all the inertias of the old regime and against vested interests ad showed that things could be changed. This later produced the creation of Romania's National Anticorruption Directorate (DNA), the agency responsible for indicting more than 1000 public officials in a single year. The DNA is being heralded for its robust approach to combatting corruption at all levels. This has been welcomed by the public who see that public malfeasance and mismanagement is being tackled and that the country is slowly coming to grips with its problems.

Things are different and have not moved at the same pace as in Romania, although they entered the EU at the same time. Bulgaria on Transparency International's latest Corruption Perceptions Index among the 28 member states of the EU has the highest perceived corruption. Romania is third worst, just ahead of Italy.

Bulgaria has been unable to tackle the nexus of oligarchs and politicians. Hristo Ivanov, who resigned as Bulgaria's justice minister last December has said "corruption in Bulgaria is not merely a matter of isolated individual actions, but of well-organized networks echeloned in the economic, political, media and judicial sectors,"

Corruption is a wide spread and deeply rooted phenomenon in the Black Sea region. In this region, corruption is a threat not only to democracy but to the states themselves, as Moldova and Ukraine stand proof. In these countries corruption has reached the maximum level, that of weakening the state and rendering its institutions dysfunctional. In a region that is eyed by Russia corruption is a high vulnerability, as it is used by this to make attempts at destabilization, influence and ultimately at control.

Russia uses corruption to infiltrate not only the political system, but especially a country's economy. Un-transparent privatization of major economic objectives allowed/allows Russia to infiltrate its capital into the economy, or to take control of enterprises it sees as competitors, and weaken them. Yet the main drive of corruption in these countries is not Russia but local elites, most of them with direct ties or the same people from the former (communist) regime.

In approaching the issue of corruption as has been said the example of Romania stands out. Four elements aligned a few years ago to embark the country on a serious anti-corruption path: external pressure, internal political will, great investigative journalism and pressure from society at large, and civil society in particular. There are other models of anti-corruption efforts, which rely less on external pressure, but for Europe's east this is an important component.

In the case of Romania, this pressure came from the EU, and other political measures, conditionality and penalties, but also, maybe more decisively, from the US, whose interest in having a reliable partner is mainly connected to its investments in security and the major role Romania plays in this.

In Ukraine the recent positive developments with the application of E-Government procedures in the field of procurement have shown how important transparency and accountability. This has saved significant funds for the public purse. Also the requirement that public officials declare their assets a month ago has caused huge interest and bewilderment (by the wealth that some public officials have amassed).

Of course we the advances that Ukraine is making there is still systemic inertia and what some call "imitation" of reforms. It is a battle royal that is ongoing and where the commitment and engagement of those forces in society and state that are for reform are fighting a relentless struggle to create a democratic political culture.

Again the importance of the transatlantic joint effort is clearly visible in supporting democratic reform efforts.

The German Marshall Fund of the United States (GMF) works on anti-corruption in the Black Sea region and focuses on the following:

- Encouraging and promoting a strong and professional investigative journalism. GMF focuses not as much on building the skills for these journalists, but on creating contacts between them so they can not only exchange and verify information, but feel better protected as part of a larger network. RISE Project is an investigative group, working in both Romania and Moldova, with an eye on Ukraine.
- Supporting civil society in its efforts to advocate and support anti-corruption activities. The role of civil society is very important in advocating for the right legal framework that not only punishes, but also prevents corruption, and for the right institutions that implement these laws (judicial system, or a dedicated part of it). GMF's Black Sea Trust for Regional Cooperation (BST) has supported advocacy efforts in Ukraine, Georgia and Moldova and exchanges of experience between these groups and their Romanian counterparts. Reform Package in Ukraine is a coalition of NGOs working on anti-corruption.
- Supporting the magistrates in carrying out their anticorruption responsibilities. GMF funded projects that trained these magistrates in Moldova, Ukraine and Georgia, and allowed for exchanges of experience between these and their Romanian counterparts (organized study tours of these people to Romania). The Expert Forum is the lead organization on this in Romania.
- Keeping anti-corruption on the agenda of these countries' international partners, as the main conditionality for further assistance. Both through grants and policy work – events, meetings with officials, study tours. One of the main messages of this effort is that a good legal framework, albeit essential, is not sufficient to ensure the success of anti-corruption efforts. As a matter of fact, passing the right laws is the easiest thing to do, and many countries in the region do have excellent laws, in general, and on anti-corruption in particular. Enforcing their provisions is what the international community needs to focus on.
- Ensuring transparency of both political and economic governance. Lack of transparency is the main condition for corruption, so ensuring transparent processes is paramount to eliminating it. Again, not only laws and regulations are important (all countries in the region have some version of the Sunshine law), but their implementation. BST supports efforts to

both pass and implement legal regulations, but also to monitor the activity of governments in all countries in the region. Fact-check in Georgia, implemented by the NGO GRASS is probably the best example, but so is the activity of Institute for Public Policy in Romania (monitoring of Parliament). One thing of major importance is privatization of major economic objectives, which journalists, civil society and international partners would need to focus on. Romania is now trying to render more transparency to these processes (perhaps a bit too late), as it has come to the realization that Russian capital has infiltrated through this process, using it to weaken certain enterprises that were in competition with the Russian ones.

The Balkans and the work of GMF's The Balkan Trust for Democracy (BTD) on anti-corruption

Wide-spread corruption is one of most significant problems for citizens of the region and an impediment to the rule of law and further democratic development. It is very difficult for civil society to address and explore cases where public money ends up in private pockets or is being misused for personal gain and very few organizations have capacities to do so.

BTD support to two prominent media outlets working solely on investigative journalism demonstrates the commitment to support initiatives working to raise awareness of citizens that there needs to be a strong public check and balance to keep government structures in Bosnia-Herzegovina and Serbia accountable and transparent in their actions. This is particularly important at a time when there are different threats to media freedom and increasing self-censorship among journalists.

Key in addressing the issue of corruption is the concerted efforts of government, civil society organizations, media and in particular investigative journalism, along with international financial and other institutions and foreign governments of the European Union in particular.

As the work and support of other donors, the support of BTD to anti-corruption efforts has resulted in broadened citizen advocacy around key issues, such as promoting state accountability and transparency, increased scrutiny of organized crime and corruption, through the Network for Affirmation of the NGO Sector's (Montenegro) monitoring of public procurement processes, the Center for Development of Media and Analysis' (Bosnia) reporting on institutional responses to cases of corruption and bribery, and the Risk Monitor Foundation's (Bulgaria) development of policy responses to organized crime in the region; and stronger civic monitoring of government performance, including through the parliamentary scorecards issued by Citizens Association MOST (Macedonia), which publicly tracked the attendance and voting records of MPs, and monitoring of implementation of laws on political and campaign spending by Centre for Democratic Transition (Montenegro), including through the efforts of Speak Up! Movement (Kosovo);

BTD has supported a number of independent media in the region, including; the Balkan Investigative Reporting Network; Production Group Mreza; Radio 100+ in Sandzak; and the Center for Investigative Journalism in Sarajevo, Internews Kosovo

The National Alliance for Local Economic Development (NALED) created a successful Business Calculator which represents a collaborative effort of all three sectors of the society and because it has a great potential to be replicated elsewhere in the region. Within this project NALED analyzed nine communal services: water supplying, channeling, taking out garbage and district heating, communal fee on firm display – "firmarina", land use fee, land development fee, market value of assets per m2 and "descriptive" property tax.

Government Accountability and Transparency-Western Balkans OGP Dialogue

The Western Balkans Open Government Partnership Dialogue organized the first regional summit on Open Government partnership (OGP) in Tirana, Albania, from September 10-11, 2015, under the title "Open Government, Engaged Citizens: A Learn-and-Show Initiative to Make Open Government Partnership work." over 250 participants attended and interacted through 20 panels.

Taking place at the Institute for Democracy and Mediation (IDM) in Tirana and co-hosted by the Albanian ministry of innovation and public administration as the Albanian OGP National Coordinator, The conference also received support from the EU, UNDP Albania, Balkan Trust for Democracy (BTD), and the U.S. Embassy to Albania. This first OGP regional gathering enabled countries of the Western Balkans to foster inclusive, accountable, transparent governance and policymaking, through enhanced civil society expertise and strengthened dialogue between civil society and their governments.

The main result of the conference was the establishment of a regional forum, whereby governments and civil society organizations (CSOs) of the Western Balkans (WB) have the opportunity to share experiences from their respective countries on improving public services, driving economic growth, reducing poverty and corruption, and restoring public faith in government. The regional approach serves to highlight good practices and successful initiatives, address the challenges faced, and establish regional support and peer-exchange mechanisms. During the two-day event, participants from the government, parliament, local government, CSOs, media and private sector have deepened their knowledge and gained the best experience with regard to different aspects of OGP implementation in their own national contexts.

In the field of government accountability and transparency the civic organization Zašto ne (Why not) works to support the development of ICT-based accountability and transparency mechanisms across Southeastern Europe, as well as regional monitoring and advocacy on the issues of open government and the promotion of civic participation. This year they hosted the fifth edition of the POINT conference (Regional Conference on Political Accountability and New Technologies) in Sarajevo. This time, an Open Data Advocacy Day was organized as an additional event to promote the need for open data from public institutions throughout the Western Balkans. This Open Data Advocacy Day showed how data can create transparency and improve the efficiency of communication between public institutions and citizens. Speakers included were government representatives, journalists, and civil society organizations (CSOs). Most importantly, all governments from the region were represented: Serbian Directorate for e-Government, OGP Task Force of the Government of Montenegro, Office for Cooperation with NGOs of Croatia, Bosnian Ministry of Justice, and the National Agency for Protection of Personal Data of Kosovo.

The main program of the POINT 4.0 conference entitled "Open Government under Construction" was launched on May 21 with the presentation of the Action SEE network. Actively supported by BTD, Action SEE is a regional network of CSOs working jointly on promoting government accountability and transparency in Southeastern Europe. The network was presented by all member organizations: from Zašto ne from Bosnia and Herzegovina, CRTA from Serbia, Metamorphosis Foundation from Macedonia, and CDT from Montenegro. They presented the network particular initiatives like: the Regional Openness Index, Instinomer, Open Parliament, and Community Booster which they implement in regular cooperation with Mjaft! from Albania, the IPKO Foundation from Kosovo, and Fundacja Techsoup from Warsaw. The conference gathered more than 150 participants from the Balkans, as well as from Europe, the U.S., the Middle East, and North Africa. The last day featured a "Datathon,"underlining the importance of data openness and the endless possibilities if data is implemented and applied within the right contexts.

Three Prime Ministers indicted for Corruption

In terms of the reality of the rule of law, its effectiveness and the reach of law there are some exemplary cases in the countries of eastern and South eastern Europe that demonstrate that no one, even the highest officials are above the law in countries of democratic transition, and all three cases come from today EU and NATO member states. These are cases significant in substantive and symbolic terms. They pave the way toward an increasingly effective judicial system as it strives to diminish the nefarious effects of corruption in society.

Adrian Nastase (Romania)

Nastase was Romania's prime minister from 200-2004 and was the first prime minister of his country to be condemned for corruption. He was convicted in 2012 to two years in prison for syphoning off funds, misuse of public money. In 2014 he was convicted to four years in prison for having accepted a bribe from a construction entrepreneur.

Ivo Sanader (Croatia)

Sanader was Croatia's Prime Minister from 2003-2009. In 2014, Zagreb county court preliminarily sentenced Sanader to nine years in prison for siphoning money from state institutions through Fimi Media marketing agency. However, the Croatian Supreme Court last year quashed the preliminary verdict, arguing that procedural errors had deprived Sanader of fair treatment, and sent back to the Zagreb county court for retrial. Sanader was accused in several corruption cases, but so far he has not been convicted in any of the cases. Croatian Constitutional Court in 2015 quashed the final ruling against Sanader in two corruption convictions -- Hypo and INA-MOL cases -- for procedural errors and ordered for retrial. Sanader was sentenced to eight years and six months in jail for allegedly taking a bribe from the Hungarian oil group MOL in 2008 to allow it to have a dominant position in Croatian state-own oil company INA, and also taking a bribe from Austria's Hypo Bank in 1994 and 1995, when he was vice foreign minister.

Janez Jansa (Slovenia)

Jansa was Prime Minister of Slovenia from 2004-2008, and 2012-2013. A conviction of corruption was unanimously overturned by the Constitutional Court on 23 April 2015. Prior to that Mr. Jansa, He was convicted of corruption and sentenced to two years in prison earlier in 2014. He has always maintained the charges were politically motivated. The constitutional court issued a temporary injunction on the prison sentence, allowing the opposition leader to pursue at large his appeal against his bribery conviction. The ruling follows the court's decision last month to restore Mr. Jansa's parliamentary seat which he secured in the July general election after the start of his prison term in late June. His seat was then suspended in October after he attended parliamentary hearings on temporary prison leaves. Mr. Jansa's bribery case, relates to the purchase of infantry armored vehicles by the Slovenian army in 2006. Mr. Jansa has denied any wrongdoing in the army procurement case and has appealed to be cleared of his conviction to the constitutional court.

A particularly high-visibility and in the eyes of some, a controversial case has been that of a Serbian businessman Miroslav Miskovic. The Special Court in Belgrade convicted him to five years for helping his son Marko Miskovic with tax evasion. The Court said Miskovic, owner of Serbian industrial giant Delta Holding, helped his son evade payment of 3 million euros in taxes. Besides the prison sentence, Miskovic will have to pay a substantial fine. In the first-instance trial, Miskovic was also charged with financial abuses related to the privatization of road maintenance companies but was acquitted of this. Serbia's prosecution for organized crime had sought a 12-year prison sentence plus fines for abuse of office and tax evasion. His defense claimed there was no evidence that he conducted financial irregularities with the road maintenance companies. Miskovic, who had been in custody for eight months before being released on bail set at 12 million euro, did not attend the verdict. His trial was delayed for health reasons at the end of last year.

His son was jailed on March 25 for three-and-a-half years in prison and fined 2.6 million euros for tax evasion in his first instance trial.

Conclusion

In a book published in 2004 Ivan Krastev, chairman of the Centre for Liberal Strategies in Sofia, Bulgaria, published a book *Shifting Obsessions: Three Essays on the Politics of Anti-Corruption*, in which without apologies for the abuses of power and misuse of public funds, offers a more skeptical reflection and some wariness to the anti-corruption policies of these past years of democratic transition. They are a sobering read with the intent and suggestion that these policies be conducted more wisely and less in the spirit of self-righteousness.

The threats to democracy today come from multiple quarters, internal and external to states. Publics are wary of their elites as populist movements on both sides of the Atlantic have demonstrated. Upholding the corpus of liberal democratic values is more important than ever in light of these challenges. Democracy and democratic freedoms have not been given to any person or society on a silver plate. They been conquered in the streets and cities of the world during the past more than two centuries and they need to be refought for every day, because there will always be those who will attempt to roll back those freedoms for their own personal gain and power.

Fighting corruption it is one of the key aspects of the defense and strengthening of democracy and democratic institutions – that it is why is important not to relent and to constantly seek efficient and effective ways to combat corruption.

The support of the United States to these processes has been crucial. The continued engagement of the US administration and of USAID remains crucial to the overall success of the democratic reform process. Working together in close cooperation with the European Union and individual European member states is essential. This will contribute to the process of consolidating democracy and help the accomplishment of the full unification of Europe in peace, and stability.

Mr. ROHRABACHER. My goodness, everybody is following the rules and 5-minute rule.

Mr. VEJVODA. Rule of law.

Mr. ROHRABACHER. Rule of law.

Sir, you may proceed.

STATEMENT OF MR. SERGEI KOLESNIKOV (FORMER CO-FOUNDER OF PETROMED HOLDING)

Mr. KOLESNIKOV. Mr. Chairman, ladies and gentlemen, I am speaking here not in the capacity of an academic or a politician, but as a person who was directly impacted by a system of the Russian corruption. Furthermore, I had a unique chance to observe this system from within and made a conscious choice not to become a part of it. I am not going to delve into details of my case, since it was well described in the article by Mr. David Ignatius of 2010, which is included in your package.

I should add that once I realized that the whole scheme was illegal and sent all the paperwork to then-President Medvedev, my life was put under threat. And if not for a timely warning, I would probably have ended up just like Sergei Magnitsky, except you would have never heard my name. I love Russia. It is my homeland. But because of my story, I was forced to leave it and live abroad.

What I would like to speak about is my firsthand experience of working closely with senior Russian officials and explain why Russian corruption is much more dangerous for the world and for the U.S. interests than corruption in Eastern and Central Europe and other nations of the world.

Indeed, corruption is all-pervasive because it is a part of the human nature. It exists in France, Great Britain, Germany, and even the United States. However, as Aristotle and Hegel pointed out, it is the category of measure which makes the key difference between good and evil.

The scale of corruption which permeated all levels of government, top down to the lowest ones, creates a perilous precedent of the major nuclear power where the whole chain of command over the weapons of mass destruction is a part of a vertically organized criminal system. Corruption in Russia is the cement which keeps the vertical of power together.

Investigation by Alexey Navalny's Fund Against Corruption, many other journalists' investigations in Russia and abroad, for example the Panama Papers, clearly demonstrated the corruptness of the Russian Government officials on all levels of power. Billions of dollars were discovered in the accounts belonging to the friends of the President, relatives of the members of the government, governors, and many other officials.

Recent broadly publicized arrests of Russian governors, police, and military generals, and even that of the minister of economy, is not an indication of an anticorruption campaign, but of an internecine fight of clans for access to the budget.

Corruption causes bad management and inept economic policies, which in turn creates social and economic instability in the superpower with nuclear weapons. Steep decline of level of life in Russia needs to be justified. The Russian Government resorted to a time-tested method of distracting its population by creating an image of an external enemy. And the enemy is the United States and its Western allies.

Two days ago, an official spokesman for the Russian Defense Ministry, General Konoshenkov, stated, to paraphrase, that the blood of the Russian servicemen is on the hands of the United States and its allies, who have created and are supporting the terrorists.

Ladies and gentlemen, I am not a politician. In the last 5 years, I have built a successful business in Europe. The reason for me accepting your invitation and speaking here is a desire to see my children's, all children's future in a safe and secure world, not imperiled by the actions of corrupt government.

Thank you very much.

[The prepared statement of Mr. Kolesnikov follows:]

Sergei Kolesnikov Written Testimony
EE&ET Subcommittee Hearing
December 7, 2016

Ladies and Gentlemen:

I am speaking here not in a capacity of an academic or a politician, but as a person who was directly impacted by a system of the Russian corruption. Furthermore, I had a unique chance to observe this system from within and made a conscious choice not to become a part of it. I am not going to delve into details of my case, since it was well described in the article by Mr. David Ignatius of 2010, which is included in your package. I should add, that once I realized that the whole scheme was illegal and sent all the paperwork to then President Medvedev, my life was put under threat, and if not for a timely warning, I would probably, have ended up just like Sergei Magnitsky, except you would have never heard my name. I love Russia, it is my homeland, but because of my story, I was forced to leave it and live abroad.

What I would like to speak about is my first hand experience of working closely with senior Russian officials, and explain why Russian corruption is much more dangerous for the world and the U.S. interests, than corruption in Eastern and Central Europe and other nations of the world.

Indeed, corruption is all-pervasive, because it is a part of the human nature. It exists in France, Great Britain, Germany, and even the United States. However, as Aristotle and Hegel pointed out, it is the category of measure, which makes the key difference between good and evil. The scale of corruption, which permeated all levels of government top down to the lowest ones, creates a perilous precedent of the major nuclear power, where the whole chain of command over the weapons of mass destruction is a part of a vertically organized criminal system. Corruption in Russia is the cement, which keeps the vertical of power together.

Investigation by Alexey Navalny's Fund Against Corruption, many other journalist investigations in Russia and abroad, for example the Panama Papers clearly demonstrated the corruptness of the Russian government officials on all levels of power. Billions of dollars were discovered in the accounts, belonging to the friends of the president, relatives of the members of the government, governors and many other officials.

Russia's ruling regime's main goal is to preserve its power at any cost, in order to continue robbing Russia and her people. Credit Swiss' research demonstrated that 110 Russian oligarchs own 35% of all Russian national riches. At that same time, none of them built their business from the ground up. They have gotten their riches by capturing natural resources or enterprises, that were created by all the Russians.

The decline in the oil prices, sanctions, that were caused by the annexation of Crimea and war in Ukraine, contraction of the national economy, have caused a significant reduction in the national budget, and as a result, intensification of the internal fighting among the various forces for the access to these resources.

Recent broadly publicized arrests of Russian governors, police and military generals and even that of minister of economy is not an indication of an anticorruption campaign, but of an internecine fight of clans for access to the budget.

Corruption causes bad management and inapt economic policies, which in turn creates social and economic instability in the superpower with nuclear weapons. Steep decline of level of life in Russia needs to be justified. The Russian authorities resorted to a time-tested method of distracting its population by creating an image of an external enemy. And the enemy is the United States and its Western allies. Two days ago an official spokesman for the Russian Defense Ministry General Konoshenkov stated, to paraphrase, that the blood of the Russian servicemen is on the hands of the United States and it's allies, who have created and are supporting the terrorists.

Ladies and Gentlemen, I am not a politician. I have built a successful business in Europe. The reason for me accepting your invitation and speaking here is a desire to see my children's, all children's future in a safe and secure world, not imperiled by the actions of corrupt authorities.

Mr. ROHRABACHER. Well, thank you, all, for your testimony today.

And I am going to let Mr. Meeks start off the questioning. Why don't you go right ahead. Okay. Well, I will go ahead then.

Mr. MEEKS. I don't interrupt the chair.

Mr. ROHRABACHER. I will take my orders from the boss over here. All right.

Well, let me ask our last witness here, when you talk about corruption in Russia, what form does that take? See, we have businessmen here who make money and then do whatever they want. They are making millions of dollars. And yet we know that there are millions of dollars coming out of Russia that are not equated to our businessmen. They would base it on some corrupt activity that they are involved in.

What is that corrupt activity that they are able to extract the wealth and then take it and deposit it somewhere else?

The INTERPRETER. Mr. Kolesnikov is going to speak Russian, and I am going to be interpreting for him if you don't mind.

Mr. ROHRABACHER. That is fine.

[The following answers were delivered through an interpreter.]

Mr. KOLESNIKOV. The main task of the Russian politicians who run the country right now today is to stay in power as long as they can. They perceive Russia as the source of their wealth; however, they prefer to live, to reside abroad, in Europe and the United States.

They are perfectly aware that their money, that their wealth can be safely protected only in a democratic country based on the rule of law. Therefore, they try, they do their best to wire their money to democratic countries, being perfectly aware that in Russia at any moment they can be taken.

Mr. ROHRABACHER. We understand that, that that is, of course, taken, and something I hope we need to deal with. He is talking about corrupt officials sending money to the West. And as I stated in the opening statement, we are going to have some focused hearings on that, whether or not American banks and Western banks and other institutions are actually accomplices with a criminal activity that is basically extracting wealth from developing countries.

The question I am asking is, you are saying that there are a large number or a certain number of officials in Russia that are engaged with corrupt activity. What is that activity that gives them the money in order to put in the Western banks?

Mr. KOLESNIKOV. The main problem of Russia is that it is a very wealthy country, and the main source of income, of revenues, are the natural resources of Russia, as well the factories and enterprises which were built by the whole Russian nation.

After the Soviet Union collapsed, practically all the properties and all the natural resources ended up in the hands of a very small group of people. And in order to pump out the money out of the country and wire to the West, you need to have control, you need to control power. In any democratic country where you have freedom of speech and free media and free elections, it would not be possible, where you have courts and when the rule of law—the law is above everything else.

Mr. ROHRABACHER. Okay. Well, let me try another approach or another thought here anyway.

When we are talking about Serbia, and you mentioned that sanctions actually led to an expansion of corruption in Serbia, so a sanctions approach to a country actually perhaps makes things worse rather than makes things better. Is that correct?

Mr. VEJVODA. Chairman, thank you for that question.

Sanctions are a double-edged sword, and any diplomat who has been engaged in this will say that. It is a kind of middle-of-the-road measure. It is without going and attacking a country for what it is doing. It doesn't want to leave that country unsanctioned or unpenalized. And thus sanctions are imposed.

When a country is under sanctions, it is obliged to somehow survive on the international market. And because there are sanctions through banks, through training, it goes underground. And there are ways in which people benefit from this, both domestically and internationally, by breaking sanctions rules.

That means internally, domestically, that everything is under control of the government. There is much less transparency or none at all in some of these dealings. And that particularly means energy imports, imports of foodstuffs. Then the customs, of course, becomes complicit because they have to let these things through without the people's right to taxation on trade being accomplished, and that then further empowers those and enriches those who are in power.

And so the reversal, once sanctions are lifted—and in the case of Serbia, sanctions were lifted only after the fall of Milosevic, it took about 10 years to do that—you then have to do all the work that any other country does in instilling the rule of law and strengthening the institutions.

Mr. ROHRABACHER. So if there is a general problem with a level of corruption in a society, for us to pick out an issue that is important to us and to put sanctions on that government in order to pressure them on a particular issue actually makes things worse in the long run?

Mr. VEJVODA. Domestically, definitely. As I said, it empowers the "elite" or those who are in power.

Mr. ROHRABACHER. Well, I hope some of my colleagues are taking that in too, because I would take this as a general rule.

And would you like to comment on that, Mr. Davidson?

Mr. DAVIDSON. Yeah. Sanctions aren't something that I have thought about a great deal or that we have really covered in our work at the Kleptocracy Initiative. But my impression, and here I wander out of my train of expertise, but it seems to me that, we take the sanctions on Russia, for instance, we are thinking more short term about weakening the economy there and dealing with a security threat as opposed to thinking of the long-term health of the society.

Certainly, sanctions are not something that can go on forever if there is going to be a healthy relationship, but in the short term it can be a very effective parry.

Mr. ROHRABACHER. Let me just note that in your testimony——

Mr. VEJVODA. Chairman, could I——

Mr. ROHRABACHER. Oh, yeah, go ahead.

Mr. VEJVODA. I would just add a few words. I am sorry.

Having lived under full sanctions—and what I am going to say is literal, that means that there were no Mickey Mouse cartoons on TV anymore, there was no Coca-Cola, it was really blanket—what happened was there was a learning curve where we eventually advocated, those of us who were in civil society fighting against the regime, was let's try and find something that has come to be called smart sanctions or rather targeted sanctions to individuals in the regime, to particular companies, to banks, et cetera, and not to have those who are actually working for democracy or freedom actually also be subject to it.

And that is what happened. The European Union, the United States then evolved in that regard. And that is how you then got individuals who were targeted, as is in the case of Russia, for example, or others.

Mr. ROHRABACHER. Let's note that in Serbia we ended up with violence and a war and mass killings that went on. In many cases, and this is a rule of thumb which I didn't include in my opening statement, is that if you take a look at some of the conflict areas of the world and some of the things that are going on, quite often, if you trace back what the root cause is, that the corruption level in those societies reached a point where large numbers of people were willing to commit acts of violence and actually get involved with more fanatic organizations, et cetera, like we saw in Serbia, where the Serbian people, who now I think are exemplary and they are doing as good a job as anybody else in Europe, they went along with horrible crimes that were being committed by their government.

So in the end, if you have corruption and it creates uncertainty among ordinary people, it can lead to the type of fanaticism that then leads to terrorism, aggression, et cetera, et cetera, which may well be seen elsewhere.

One last point, and then I am going to let Mr. Meeks take over here.

Mr. Davidson, you made a point that children of the crooks and their families eventually, if someone is part of a criminal syndicate in a country, eventually they have so much money that they eventually become part of the elite cultural people of that society. They are the prominent citizens after one or two generations.

Let me just note that this doesn't happen in those countries; that has happened in our country. How many people in prominent families started out here as slavers? They sold slaves, that despicable act that even where it was legal in the South, they thought that was a despicable profession to be in. But yet, people emerged. Bootleggers and people involved in gangster families in our country have after one or two generations become prominent citizens. And so what you are saying is not something that we should be just pointing over there; we have got to understand that that is a cycle that happens here.

Today, what I am very concerned about is not the children and not the prominent families in the future that this will create, but instead how we have perhaps institutions in our society that are respectable institutions that are being utilized by especially foreign corrupt officials and gangsters in other societies.

I mean, how many people are making real estate deals with criminals now in our country? And those criminals may not well be Americans. They may be Russians or they could be Chinese or they could be any number of countries that come here to launder their money, and yet we have our very respectable and prominent citizens engaged in what would have to be an accomplice to a crime.

So anyway, Mr. Meeks, you may proceed, and we will have a second round of questions afterwards for everybody.

Mr. MEEKS. Thank you, Mr. Chairman.

Very interesting. I want to thank the witnesses for their testimony and I am going to try to go through everybody real quickly.

Maybe I will start with you, Mr. Davidson, and just trying to figure out, moving forward first, how are corruption and populism related in Europe? And what examples can you provide that would be helpful to monitor corruption in 2017 as we move forward? Because a lot is going on in Europe right now, politically and otherwise, and corruption could do something that indeed could destroy the democratic countries, many of whom are allies.

So I was wondering if you could just tell us what could be helpful. How can we monitor what is going on in 2017 so that we can be—it could be helpful as we deal with our allies over here?

Mr. DAVIDSON. Okay. That is a tough question. I will take a shot at it.

I think if we look at populism in Europe, and we can relate that to populism in our country too perhaps, but certainly when you have corruption—well, let's take—Ukraine would be a sort of exaggerated example of this. If people feel that the political leadership is corrupt and that they can't trust their leaders, they turn to populism, very simply. So I think that is what we are seeing.

Mr. MEEKS. Do you want to say, Mr. Vejvoda?

Mr. VEJVODA. Yeah, it is definitely not an easy question, because what we see in populism is a kind of a perfect storm where there has been resilience and patience on the number of people who have been the losers of globalization.

And yet, it is strange, because if you take Germany, for example, it is one of the countries where there is the lowest level of unemployment, where they have high income in the working class, and yet there is a populist movement because there is a fear of migration, what it will do to the cultural identity of Germans. And so the so-called—the party called Alternatives for Germany, Alternative fur Deutschland, is capitalizing on that fear.

I was in Berlin in January and then just last week. And in January, members of the German Parliament told me: You must understand that there is a sense of panic in this country with this wave of migration that is coming in, that the government has lost control, and that, simply, there will be a wave of people in German cities.

Now, that has come under control, as you know, through the agreement between the European Union and Turkey. But the various segments of and reasons of why there is a populist movement are not solely in that case linked to issues of corruption. In Ukraine, it is definitely different, as was mentioned.

So I think one needs to look at a country-by-country basis, fully understand that there is something common in the transatlantic arena as we watch these movements rise.

Mr. MEEKS. And you said something, and I get concerned, I think that Mr. Rohrabacher was probably right in certain things here even in the United States, because I get concerned that we may be turning into an oligarchy country, when you look at the number of folks with money and the financing. I think one of you mentioned the financing of political parties.

And I look at how our political parties, both sides are financed now by the ultra-1 percent, et cetera. To me, those are warning signs. So I don't to point a finger over there if there is something similar happening here and how that leads to whether it is populism or leads to a scenario where you have a strong-armed person that becomes the head of state or something of that nature.

And then at the same time you asked the question, Mr. Davidson, what can we do? And you had a certain thing. So I want to hear, what do you think we can do?

Mr. Vejvoda, you said that sanctions is not something that works. I mean, from my perspective, it depends upon how, because I look at then, what do you do if not sanctions? Is there a special type of sanctions? Or what do you do?

I look at, from my perspective, not in Europe, but the success that sanctions had in a place like South Africa to bring down a regime that was full of apartheid and injustices, et cetera.

So the question then is, what do you do? You can't sit by and do nothing. What would you say we do?

Start with Mr. Davidson.

Mr. DAVIDSON. Starting with me?

Well, I will mention some of the other points that are in my testimony then. And just to underscore again the role of what I like to call anonymous companies in terms of, if we just think about Europe and the countries, the territory we have been focusing on, and corrupt officials bringing money out of those countries into the West, it is usually via the use of so-called shell companies, anonymous companies. So the ownership is concealed, and these are the vehicles used for purchasing real estate to a great extent.

In London, it is quite dramatic. There is some unbelievable number of expensive apartments and homes that are owned by shell companies, and nobody knows who really owns them, except we do, in some cases, because some of the really large ones, you see people going in and out of them now and it is reported on and stuff.

But this is the low-hanging fruit right now is the anonymous shell company for corruption, very broadly, including the United States. I mean, when you want to hide something you are going to use an anonymous shell company.

The second thing I have in my testimony, Mr. Meeks, is a little vague, one might say. But if we look at the offshore financial system and all the secrecy we provide, anonymous shell companies are one aspect of it, but there are all these smaller things, the blocking and tackling that we could do. And consulting experts at Treasury, at DOJ would be the way to go with that to get into more detail on it, I would think.

And we have some very good things going on right now with our law enforcement agencies. The FBI has this relatively new group that started in January 2015, the international anticorruption squad. And the original name for it had the word ''kleptocracy'' in there somewhere and now they have renamed it. And they are doing some very good work. Because of the power of our financial system and this almost trek that stuff sometimes has to go through New York, we can reach quite far in terms of taking anti-kleptocratic measures.

And I won't mention the last point in my testimony because it is not really germane to your question, but the Global Magnitsky Act, for instance, has a provision in there that could give a lot of discretion to our government in terms of going after people for human rights abuses or—I mean, we have a lot of discretion there. So that is also something that could be part of the toolkit.

Mr. VEJVODA. Thank you for your question, Congressman.

I didn't say that sanctions don't work. I said they are a double-edged sword. They have an effect that one wants to reach if one imposes sanctions, but they have a second face to them which is the internal corruption of society and state. And so I think it is finding that balance, and that is why I talked about this search for smart sanctions, targeting individuals, certain companies, et cetera.

In the case of Serbia, there was also this loose talk, as we heard in Russia when sanctions were just imposed: Oh, this will not have an effect, don't worry, we will be able to do it. But they do. They do have economic effect, as you mentioned, in South Africa; they were very effective in Cuba, as we know also, for many years. So they definitely hit like a radiation, maybe it is a scattershot that touches too many, has too many effects.

So, yeah, I think one has to keep drilling down. And we have a number of examples internationally of sanctions, and I think much has been learned from the various examples that have been mentioned.

I would also like to mention the case of Switzerland in regards to what Charles Davidson was saying about the banking secrecy in Switzerland and the pressure that the U.S. Government put on for many years for that secrecy to be revealed, because so many people from all over the world were putting their assets and their finances into. And Switzerland has had to come out and sign agreements on sharing information, both with the U.S., of course, and the European Union.

And so I think that is an example of the way to go to uncover the shell companies and, as one would say colloquially, follow the money, but then see where the money is being held and hidden and so that light is shed into those places where these people actually find ways where the money is laundered, where their assets are kept.

And Charles Davidson is right to mention London, which has been mentioned so many times over these past several years as a place where banks and institutions have profited.

And the agencies, the various agencies of the U.S. Government, of course Treasury Department, are key through their investigative roles in finding where actually the paths and the dynamics in which this corrupt money finds its way on the international arena.

And I would add that the international financial institutions play a key role, whether it is the International Monetary Fund, the World Bank, European Bank for Reconstruction and Development, who approve, of course, loans, or the various ways in which aid is given, but before that aid is given, countries need to accede to certain conditions and comply with certain conditions before money is sent.

Mr. KOLESNIKOV. I would like to point out that there is a very simple and clear mechanism to fight corruption, which is to provide the population with the truth, with the true information.

In Russia, this doesn't exist today. The majority of Russians consume their information from TV, and the TV channels never, ever reveal any cases of serious corruption among the government and the people close to the government. Instead, the TV channels every day nails in the head of Russians the same message, that our life gets worse, it is not our fault, it is not because of us, it is because of the external enemy. And today, they have chosen this enemy, which is the United States.

This is a very dangerous trend because many people in Russia today sincerely believe that the United States and European countries are true enemies of Russia.

Ten years ago or 5 years ago nobody could have even fathomed the idea that there are going to be tank battles in the center of Europe and 10,000 people are going to be killed in fighting in Ukraine. However, it happened, and it happened because the information channels created the picture of an enemy.

Many Russians sincerely volunteered to go to Ukraine and fight against Nazis, against fascism. We live today in a very interesting new world where information wars are becoming no less dangerous than real wars. You have two options. You can kill a man or you can change his mentality, you can change his consciousness, and the effect is going to be the same.

And referring to the sanctions, I should say, yes, the sanctions have a great impact on Russia today. And my only point is that any sanctions should have a very specific goal. If they are vague and ambiguous, they are not clear.

Mr. ROHRABACHER. Thank you very much.

Mr. Weber.

There will be a second round of questions.

Mr. WEBER. Thank you, Mr. Chairman.

Mr. Vejvoda, you said political losses become economic winners in the new economy because they have insider information. So what you are seeing is a government, a country in turmoil, where it is going down because of the corruption, and yet the very ones who caused it to go down actually become the economic winners in the new order, if you will. Fix that for me.

Mr. VEJVODA. Fix that?

Mr. WEBER. Uh-huh.

Mr. VEJVODA. Well, it is being fixed more or less successfully, and has been fixed, for example, in the Baltic countries. In Poland there are mixed results. And then you go to scale, Moldova is probably at the other end in this region of the world that I know best, which is Central and Eastern Europe and southeastern Europe, the Balkans.

Mr. WEBER. But what do you do, specifics, how do you prevent that from happening?

Mr. VEJVODA. Well, the prevention, as I said, requires, to put it simply, a holistic approach, it requires what the people of Maidan did.

Mr. WEBER. Holistic or ballistic?

Mr. VEJVODA. Holistic.

Mr. WEBER. Okay. I missed that.

Mr. VEJVODA. We are not going ballistic here.

Society awakens to the fact that it has the freedom to actually voice its desire to have an orderly society based on democracy. That does not happen overnight. Rome was not built in a day.

And we are seeing that even though many of us had illusions that it would go quicker in some of our countries, it has taken more time and there are twists and turns, as we see, for example, in Hungary, where there has been a regression of democracy over the past several years.

But, by and large, the countries that have come out of communism have step by step moved and created democratic institutions, instilled them with habits of the heart that are a democratic political culture. And since democracy is not given on a plate, it needs to be conquered every day.

And thus, people need to be vigilant to the fact that there are those who want to take on more power and rich, because in the end, many of these—at least the war in the former Yugoslavia was about retaining power. And populism and nationalist feelings were used for that power-retention strategy, which took us down the hellhole of war from which we recovered 10 years later, the different parts of Yugoslavia.

Mr. WEBER. Yeah. Let me ask you this. I think you compared and contrasted, was it Yugoslavia and Poland or was it Ukraine——

Mr. VEJVODA. Ukraine and Poland.

Mr. WEBER. Okay.

Mr. VEJVODA. That is an example, a comparison that so many people, economists, political scientists, use today to show how divergent these paths can be from an equal starting point.

Mr. WEBER. So Poland, the process in Poland good, the process in Ukraine bad?

Mr. VEJVODA. Yeah.

Mr. WEBER. Why? What is the difference?

Mr. VEJVODA. Well, the difference was that there wasn't this effort at structural democratic reform that Poland went through beginning with 1990—or rather 1989—when they had their first——

Mr. WEBER. Is that because somebody stepped up to the plate and took the lead on that?

Mr. VEJVODA. Absolutely. Leaders like Lech Walesa, who, as you know, spoke here in front of the Congress, and others who were determined, one, to return to Europe and correct the division of Europe that happened, the embrace by the European Union and the United States, the support that they got in these efforts from agencies like USAID.

Mr. WEBER. So what you are describing is a political will married to individual courage.

Mr. VEJVODA. Absolutely. And that is what we did not see in Ukraine. Even though there was an enormous hope after the Orange Revolution when everyone hoped, Ukrainian citizens first and foremost, that finally they had got the courageous leaders backed by the political will of the people to do it, it is mildly put to say that there was huge disappointment, because these leaders of the Orange Revolution turned out to be involved in the same corrupt activities.

Mr. WEBER. All right. Well, thank you.

Let me move on. I know I am getting over my time. And so let me go to Mr. Kolesnikov.

You have a successful business in Europe, true?

Mr. KOLESNIKOV. Yes.

Mr. WEBER. Did you have one in Russia?

Mr. KOLESNIKOV. Yes.

Mr. WEBER. Did you lose it?

Mr. KOLESNIKOV. Yes.

Mr. WEBER. But you took those business principles that you learned in Russia and you applied them in Europe.

Mr. KOLESNIKOV. I brought with me my skills and my experience, which is the crucial thing in business. If you manage to build a business, successful business, in such a difficult country like Russia, in a normal democratic country, it is way easier than that.

Mr. WEBER. Should that be incentive enough for someone to have the political will and marry it to that individual courage I talked about and make a better life, not just for them, but for their kids and their grandkids and the rest of the country?

Mr. KOLESNIKOV. I can assure you that today the true entrepreneurs in Russia, people who build a business with their own hands and their brains, using their own skills and experience, their biggest dream is to have democracy in Russia where the courts are working properly and when the law is observed.

Mr. WEBER. Okay. Welcome to the American Dream.

Mr. KOLESNIKOV. You know that probably you are perfectly aware that many Russian business people, scientists, researchers, they actually found in the United States a second home.

Mr. WEBER. Well, it is what I like to say, all the smart Russians over in Russia ain't over in Russia, they are over here.

But let me end with this. How do you communicate to people in Russia that that American Dream, democracy, capitalism, free enterprise, is worth the risk and the price? When you do that, you will have enough people that will rise up and take that country.

Mr. KOLESNIKOV. You touched a very important issue, but today there is a very simple situation. Those of us, those people who would like to explain to Russians how it works and why it is worth, they have no ability, no opportunity to say that. In Russia, as I said earlier, the government, the corrupt government controls all the TV channels, which from dusk to dawn try to instill the same idea into the heads of Russian people: It is not our fault that we have bad life, it is enemies, external enemy. And the idea of the enemy is repeated over and over in talk shows and all kinds of different TV programs.

Mr. WEBER. Who was it that said the pen is mightier than the sword? Apparently he had never been in a sword fight.

Well, thank you for being here today. You have your work cut out for you.

Mr. KOLESNIKOV. Thank you very much.

Mr. ROHRABACHER. All right. Thank you all. And we are going to have a second round of questions if anybody would like to join us in that, and I will start that off.

Let me just note about the talk of sanctions and the idea that aiming sanctions at specific corrupt and human rights-abusing government officials is not a bad idea. I actually voted against it, however, because—and we are talking about the Magnitsky Act—because I happen to believe that naming it the Magnitsky Act was wrong.

Because yet to prove—there are a lot of questions about that particular case, and those questions need to be answered before we compromise with our level of insistency on what we insist on for what is truth or not and what is a true crime. And the Magnitsky Act should not have been named that. And I am the only one who voted against it. I know my ranking member and I disagreed on this.

But in terms of actually sanctioning individual government officials throughout the world who are engaged in some type of torture or anti—well, doing things that we would not accept here as acceptable, killing prisoners or committing acts of torture, et cetera, the human rights abuses.

So with that said, I agree with that assessment. We should be focusing on those individuals. And, again, however, I think the Russians were mistreated in the Magnitsky case, because that title of that bill is maybe suggesting that something was done that has not been proven yet. So, anyway, that is just a thought.

I think that we have to also note, we have oligarchs here. We have oligarchs in the United States. Many of them happen to be technology developers, okay, they came up with a new type of technology, they earned billions of dollars on it. And whether it is PayPal or whatever, or some type of new medical device or whatever, they made their money honestly.

And the question is, however, in some countries, then, for an oligarch to take the money and transfer it outside the society is illegal, and that is where an oligarch becomes a corrupt person, okay?

Is that what we are talking about here when we talk about oligarch corruption? Because our oligarchs do that. Our billionaires, multibillionaires, they take money out of the country and put it in banks and different investments overseas all the time. Maybe I will ask all of you on that question.

Let's start with Mr. Davidson. How does that add up? That is not what we are talking about here, is it?

Mr. DAVIDSON. No. Mr. Chairman, I think it is sort of a fun question too in a way.

Mr. ROHRABACHER. Yes, I like to have fun at these hearings.

Mr. DAVIDSON. Yeah. No, fun is great. And I think it is a very good question, because what is an oligarch, really? And we sort of throw the term out there toward a lot of people.

If we were to try to—I am just going to take a shot, just I am thinking aloud as to what an oligarch could be in the U.S. context. And very often when we use it in the European context, the territory that is our designated zone today, these are people who have seized monopolies in most cases on a given industry.

So if we wanted to translate that into the U.S., what we would see with a lot of these technology entrepreneurs is indeed, I mean, they haven't done anything wrong, they just happen to have been so successful, they end up with a monopoly.

Mr. ROHRABACHER. Right.

Mr. DAVIDSON. And for that we have had antitrust in the past, which, of course, is not—perhaps it has been enforced more forcefully at times than it is right now, but it was used, of course, by Teddy Roosevelt in a big way to revolutionize our country, really. So was John D. Rockefeller an oligarch? I mean, I guess by that definition you might say yes.

I detect a little bit of a notion in your question that some of these technology oligarchs have become too powerful in their given markets. If that is the case, it seems to me we do have the antitrust laws and ways that we could look at that.

The problem we have, it seems to me, in the technology area is that a lot of these technology verticals are kind of natural monopolies. So I don't know how we would——

Mr. ROHRABACHER. Well, there are some oligarchs that have— you can receive great government subsidies for whatever business practice they decided to go for. And did they impact the legislative or the executive branch people who were making the decision as to how much subsidy this or that would get?

There are very serious questions when we start pointing fingers at other people. And as I say—look, I was designated about 2 years ago as the poorest Member of Congress, okay? Well, I am a happy man, and I am not someone who is resentful that somebody else has more. Sometimes I think that we teach people that we should resent them.

And let me just note, of the billionaires in this country, Mr. Meeks, the vast majority supported your candidate for President, not mine. They did an analysis of the billionaires, and Hillary had a lot more than Trump, but Trump himself is a billionaire.

So we can't just say because someone has a lot of money, that they are an oligarch, which then says that they are evil in some way. However, let me note that, and back to Russia.

And Russia had a problem in the beginning, and one of the major problems was that money left that country and went into European and American financial institutions.

We talk about England. Correct me if I am wrong, Mr. Davidson, but if someone transfers some money from Russia or from anywhere else into a bank in England, do they have that same rule that they can loan out 10 times the amount of money that they actually have on deposit?

So what have we done? We have enriched England or that bank enormously by having that money going from Russia or wherever else into that bank in England. And, of course, what the bank in England provides is safe haven for people who want to get away from paying taxes and having that wealth controlled by the government in the country where they made that money.

This is problematic, and I really believe that many of the situations that we have now that was described in Russia can be traced back to, yes, when Russia should have been prospering and it was going through this period, we ended up having the wealth taken out, which actually made it 10 times more difficult for them to have a stronger economy.

And then we know now also that sanctions directed at Russia did not work, do not work in the long-run. Let me note that there is a bank in—is it Sberbank, is that what they call it, in Russia? Sberbank, when we visited Russia last and talked to the various leaders in the banking community, they were saying they followed every single rule that they were asked to follow, and yet there are sanctions against them that have impacted them in a negative way.

So targeting sanctions is very important if we expect those people in these various countries to actually pay attention, to be supportive, and to cut out the type of corruption that we are talking about today.

So I guess I have had my say. You guys, maybe you want to comment on some of the things I just said, and then we will move on. Again, I voted against the Magnitsky Act, but only because of the title. The idea of targeting individuals for human rights abuses in those countries is a good idea. And when and if they prove that case in terms of Magnitsky, then I will change my position on that bill, but until then, I thought it was a gratuitous slap at Russia.

And one last thought. I know I disagree with my colleagues here, but, no, we have had many gratuitous slaps at Russia, where things are just as bad over here, or over there, whether we are talking about oligarchs or whatever, manipulating the system and extracting wealth from the system. We have our oligarchs here, and we have lots of things that we do here that are being done over there and being labeled in a very hostile, pejorative way, and by people who actually want to have bad relations with Russia for whatever reason.

So with that said, and maybe each witness can have a minute to refute everything I just said or to agree with it or whatever. Mr. Davidson, do you want to start?

Mr. DAVIDSON. Sure. No, I don't have anything to add to that. I agree with most of it. And I agree no one has a monopoly on virtue in general when we have looked at the enabling role of the West in this whole problem, which is central.

Now, you brought up also what happened in the 1990s in Russia and the role that was played. I mean, there are some very interesting things, we don't have time to get into that, but that could be a whole hearing, of course, unto itself.

Mr. ROHRABACHER. Well, we do have, for example, take the reason why we call it the Magnitsky Act. And the case, that I believe is yet to be settled, is based on an American who went to Russia, made billions of dollars off the economic turmoil, and then left the country and was able to take his money out of the country. And Magnitsky was his accountant. And the question is, is whether or not he paid the $250 million in taxes that were due from the billions of dollars that he had earned in that chaotic situation in Russia.

Now, that is the heart of that case. Did the jailers of Mr. Magnitsky kill him because they were being afraid that he would finger them for that $250 million that they had some way managed to change the bookkeeping that they were able to keep or was he roughed up and maybe killed because he wouldn't say where that $250 million owed to the Russian government was? That is the whole crux of the matter, and it is yet to be determined which of those stories.

But with that said, again, targeting corrupt officials, targeting human rights abusers specifically is a good thing as far as I am concerned.

Yes, sir.

Mr. DAVIDSON. May I just comment on that, Mr. Chairman? Well, the whole story surrounding Magnitsky and all is a very good read. Bill Browder's book, ''Red Notice,'' is at least as good as any of the John le Carre. So quite a story. And it is incredibly intricate and complicated also, which sort of can be obfuscating in terms of how one approaches the issue.

But I thought it was very interesting the way you support the principles of the bill and all of that. And I think it was silly—it was a mistake to call it the Magnitsky Act, because it makes it sound too personal, as though it is some vendetta or something like that, when in fact it is a general principle for which there has been huge support in the Congress and the Senate.

Mr. ROHRABACHER. And it was a specific slap at Russia, which would make people think maybe this is just Russian situation of human rights abuses, and it was not. It was aimed at a general thing.

Anyway, I just wanted to make sure I am on the record as to why I voted against that particular situation. I don't think gratuitously slapping Russia around is going to make things better.

Sir.

Mr. VEJVODA. Mr. Chairman, thank you very much. Just, obviously, no one has the monopoly on virtue, but I think as democracy and capitalism evolved, there was an understanding that there is a need to put boundaries to wealth, respecting the full freedom of entrepreneurship, and that is what has made the West writ large successful, because of that freedom of speech, of enterprise, of association.

And so when one speaks of oligarchs or simply wealthy people in the United States or Europe, it is the fact that they have to pay taxes. And obviously some of them try to avoid it by going to shell companies or sending their money abroad.

Mr. ROHRABACHER. Or giving campaign donations and making regulations that eliminate their tax liability or getting a large subsidy from the government.

Mr. VEJVODA. Yeah. Well, Citizens United, as you know, is a contentious question here: Is money good in politics or bad? In Europe, there are limits, as you know, and parties get money from the Parliament and private money is not involved. So that is a whole very big and, I think, important issue for the type of polity and political framework that we all have.

But I think the key thing here is really, again, the rule of law. And I think if, as Mr. Kolesnikov said, people who have money would rather have the rule of law where they can keep the money in their own national bank rather than have to have it somewhere else, I think it is that fear or threat of racketeering.

There are countries where people are very successful business people, and then the government, because of the lack of the rule of law or authoritarian structure, simply say, "Well, okay, you have made this money now; now we take over," and you are lucky if you save your life, and go do business elsewhere. So I think that is really the major difference between these authoritarian countries and the others where there is a democratic system based on the rule of law.

Mr. KOLESNIKOV. If we are going to be referring to the Magnitsky law, I believe that this is a more powerful tool than a bunch of nuclear submarines which the United States has in the world oceans, because this is the first specific language which says that if a government official steals money or violates human rights, he or she could be punished. It is not assured that he is going to be punished, but can be punished.

Mr. ROHRABACHER. Absolutely right.

Mr. KOLESNIKOV. The Magnitsky case is not that difficult. The taxes were paid, but then the taxes were stolen from the national budget by investigators, by people who put Magnitsky in jail.

Mr. ROHRABACHER. That is the charge, and there are two different points of view on that. But that certainly is what the other side to that is saying.

Mr. KOLESNIKOV. I agree that the business which Mr. Browder made his billions in Russia was not pretty, but he did it in a legal way, and he did pay his taxes, and then he removed his money out of Russia, probably because he sensed some kind of threat that he might not be able to take this money.

Again, I am not saying that I find Mr. Browder's business in Russia pretty, but we should make it very clear, was it legal or illegal?

Mr. ROHRABACHER. By the way, again, I am not suggesting Mr. Browder is guilty or innocent. I am saying that what you are saying now has not been proven one way or the other, and thus, to put his name on the bill that holds public officials accountable for human rights abuses and name it that under this Russian case was a gratuitous slap at Russia before that case has actually determined whether or not the truth—where the truth lies.

So I am very happy to have you express that opinion. There are other opinions as well that perhaps the opposite is true from what you said. That is what we need to find out.

But still it is the principle of the case, which is—which we all agree on, you agree on, we agree on—hold specific officials accountable rather than making some generalized attack on a particular country.

Mr. KOLESNIKOV. Well, the name of this act, after all, is just a name. What counts is the essence. Eventually you can change the title any time.

Mr. ROHRABACHER. Well, we might. We might do that someday.

Well, thank you very much for being with us today.

And, Mr. Meeks, you have the final words here.

Mr. MEEKS. Thank you, Mr. Chairman.

Let me just ask—where do I want to start? I am going to start with Mr. Kolesnikov. Did you ever experience any intimidation either before you released your information or after, or now any in your regular walk of life?

Mr. KOLESNIKOV. The reason why I left Russia was specifically because I was alerted that the false accusations were going to be trumped up against me. The drugs were supposed to be placed in my car, I was supposed to be arrested for possession of drugs, put in jail, and then you can easily figure out what could happen to me in jail. And the reason why it should have had happened was because I rejected to work in this illegal framework where I was suggested to take part.

After I sent the documents to—all the paperwork to President Medvedev and they became public, I got many threats. But there is only so much you can do about it. It was my civic duty, it was the position of a citizen and patriot of my country, and I do not regret what I did.

Mr. MEEKS. Were you ever an associate of President Putin's?

Mr. KOLESNIKOV. Yes.

Mr. MEEKS. Could you tell us how or if he had any involvement in any of this or how he rationalized this?

Mr. KOLESNIKOV. The Petromed case is quite in detail described on my Web site and the articles written about my case, and anybody who is—because there are too many details, anybody can check and see it. It is going to take about 15, 20 minutes for me to provide all the details about the case, which I am afraid is going to be too long for this venue. And Mr. Ignatius in his article set out most crucial elements of this case. If you have any specific questions, I am ready to answer.

Mr. MEEKS. Thank you, and we will. And I would love to come back and have a further dialogue. I know we are running out of time. I just wanted to ask Mr. Davidson and Mr. Vejvoda a couple of ending questions also, because it has been a great hearing, and I am listening and learning, et cetera.

The question that comes into my mind now is, given what we have heard, is what does success even look like in the fight against corruption? What would you say? Can you give me an example, what does success look like? How can we make a determination if we are being successful?

And I add that on, for example, we currently have sanctions against Russia. Is that successful? Is it not? Should we alter it? What do you think it looks like?

Mr. VEJVODA. Thank you, Congressman Meeks, for those questions. Specifically on that last one, I think, having lived in a country that was under sanctions, they take time and they drill and they work and they cause pain to the economy, because you are not fully open. Of course, a country like Russia can impose countersanctions, which a small country like Serbia could not, and so there is pain in certain parts of the European economy. But as open, democratic, capitalist societies, they find easier ways in which they can reorient their trade.

So, yeah, I mean, the answer is yes, I think they are effective. As we said at the beginning, or I said, they are a double-edged sword. They have diverse effect. And as diplomats will say, this is a kind of middle-of-the-road measure when you don't want to go to war and on the other hand you don't want to do anything. It is something in between.

What is the measure of success? I think, as we all agree, there is corruption in every society, even the most democratic. I guess in a Sweden or wherever, you will find examples. I remember the case of former Chancellor Helmut Kohl, the unifier of Germany in the beginning of the 1990s, he was caught with his hand in the party slush fund of the Christian Democratic Union. That was quite a well-known case. I think of Enron here in the U.S. or things like that. There are things that spring forward.

But I think the measure is really how high or low the level of corruption is. I don't think one can eliminate it. There is something in human nature where people will try and skew the rules. You have British parliamentarians who have abused the moneys they have used. I don't want to mention any names here, but some of them have actually gone to jail. Your colleagues in Westminster simply paid out of what was supposed to be for their staffers for a house aid or their garden or some home improvement. So that shows that even if you live in a democratic country, you are not immune to that.

So I would simply say that the lower the level of corruption, the more successful we are in actually tackling it. And, again, it is something like democracy itself. One needs to work at it every day to have the agencies of government, to have the supervisors of the supervisors at customs posts, the various agencies, to oversee whether things are being done appropriately. And, of course, the taxation system that needs to oversee the fact is everyone actually paying their fair deal, and I would say more for those who are wealthier disproportionately than at the other end, but the law is equal for everyone.

Mr. MEEKS. Mr. Davidson.

Mr. DAVIDSON. What would success look like? Well, certainly less corruption, and that we all agree to, but it also means on a sustained basis. So it is not something where we can sort of parachute in for a bit and, well, any number of means to improve things for a bit in one country, and then get out, and things fall apart. We have tried to do that in a few cases, not in Europe, but elsewhere, of course, and it is a dramatic failure and costs us a ton of money.

But I think success really is about changing the global financial system in terms of secrecy and providing a safe haven for corrupt people with political power when there has been state capture in particular.

Now, one of the effects, if we push the money back into the country, at a minimum things will be better. So the resources, instead of the $150 million house in London, you will have that $150 million in the country. People can argue over it. It will get invested somehow. Even if it is buying Rolls-Royces, whoever is servicing those Rolls-Royces in the garage down the street will have a job at least, as opposed to starving.

So I think we need to force the money back into these countries by cleaning up our own act and ceasing to shelter the assets.

Mr. MEEKS. I think my last, because I talked a lot about Russia, but I also wanted to just ask a question quickly about Ukraine.

Vice President Biden described corruption as eating Ukraine like a cancer; eating Ukraine like a cancer. How is the Government of Ukraine, if you have any ideas, working to fight this cancer? And what do you think are the stumbling blocks to it being successful?

Mr. VEJVODA. If I may start. I was in Ukraine just at the beginning of November when they voted in the electronic government, e-government element on procurements. And this is one of the key—one of many measures that needs to be implemented in many places, because it simply makes the procurement process, governmental procurement process transparent. And people can follow on the Web sites, rather than in dark rooms, where deals are made and deals are made much more difficult, if not impossible, if you have an e-procurement system.

The other thing that has been positive is that Ukrainian officials have had to declare their assets, all of them. And the punishments or penalties if they do not that were pretty high, and so everyone declared their assets. Now, the surprise was that many parliamentarians declared that they had 10 apartments or 10 cars or whatever, and so the Ukrainian people suddenly were a bit in shock and awe because their representatives suddenly, they realized, had made money in ways that are not appropriate.

So as in any country, I would say that Ukraine is doing a lot to clean up their act, to put it colloquially, but on the other hand, the old habits are not going away so quickly. And the various levels of corruption, and I think Vice President Biden rightly spoke in those terms about a cancer, and it is a battle royal that is going on for, to put it poetically, the soul of Ukraine, while they are at war, while they are in a situation where a part of their territory has been taken by Russia, contrary to all international law, and where there is the conflict in the east where Russia is involved in various ways. So it is like reforming, you know, repairing a ship in a high storm.

But, again, this is really a test case where, with the support of the United States, of the European Union, and the European Union is putting equally a lot of money into Ukraine and their reforms, and I would say that this needs to be pursued, even though there are these difficulties that everyone perceives, and keep the feet to the fire of the elected Ukrainian officials to pursue these efforts.

There will be setbacks, but if the vector is recognizably in the good direction, I think we should, as the West, support this country that wants—and, again, the Maidan was a clear signal that the people of Ukraine do want to change.

I would add to what Charles Davidson said, that it was about corruption, which it absolutely was, but it was also about the fact that the Ukrainians thought that their government was taking them to the European Union. The day that Yanukovych, former President Yanukovych, decided not to sign that next step to the European Union, that is when Maidan started.

So it was a coincidence of two things. If we feel, as the people of Ukraine, that you are taking us to Europe, however slowly you are moving, we are okay, and we know that you are corrupt and we will clean this up. But the day that Yanukovych, said, no, we are not going to Europe, that is when all the European flags came onto the Maidan. So I think it is important to understand those two things.

Mr. DAVIDSON. Well, regarding Ukraine, I think the institutionalized corruption at the top seems daunting, and we don't seem to have seen much progress lately with that. And I avoided using the "K" word there. I will leave it at institutionalized corruption.

I would go back to what Congressman Weber said earlier in terms of Ukraine. And in terms of their leadership, I think they need political will and individual courage.

Mr. MEEKS. Thank you.

Mr. KOLESNIKOV. I should say that I see eye to eye with Mr. Vejvoda. I completely agree. And I have been to Ukraine three times this year, and I have very close relations with my Ukrainian business partners.

The key difference between Ukraine and Russia is, number one, there is true real freedom of speech in Ukraine, they have true real elections in Ukraine, and they have real civil society in Ukraine, which took shape now and which does not want to live in a corrupt society.

I spoke to many Ukrainians on the street, and they are completely different than Russians because they freely express their opinions. They openly admit that, yes, we have corrupt government officials, yes, we have corrupt legislators, we are perfectly aware of it, but we can change the situation and we will change the situation. That is the biggest difference.

Mr. ROHRABACHER. Well, I would like to thank all of our witnesses. Just a couple thoughts. And let me just note, I was there during the Orange Revolution. I actually camped out in Maidan in the tents they had there. It was cold, I might add.

And let me just note that Cathy Chumachenko, who worked with me in the Reagan White House, turned out to be first lady, and she and her husband, who came into power after that, the Orange Revolution, as has been indicated in the testimony, their administration was so corrupt that the people of Ukraine ended up voting for Yanukovych in the next election.

And Yanukovych, I might add, was democratically elected, OSCE verified it. However, he didn't leave office in a democratic election. He left office because there was a violent revolution that started in Maidan right after he decided to go with the European Union. And there are discussions about whether the European Union was indeed interfering with what was going on.

But let me just say this, that had Yanukovych not been overthrown or not been kicked out with violent demonstrations in the Maidan, that he would have been kicked out in the next election. There is no doubt. He was corrupt and he was doing things that the public didn't like, and the very next election he would have been kicked out. And had they waited to kick him out rather than overthrow him 2 years earlier than the free election demanded, I do not believe that any of this horror story that we faced in the last couple years in Ukraine would have happened. You would have had a peaceful transfer of power, which is what they should have had.

Yanukovych deserved to be removed by his people, because he was as corrupt as the people who he replaced, who were as corrupt as the people they replaced. And I am not sure how that bodes well in the future for Ukraine, because the information I am getting now is that the current government is also deeply engaged in corrupt practices and the sending of large amounts of money to European banks.

So with that said, let's pray that that problem will some way be relieved from the poor suffering Ukrainians, who I don't know any other people in the 20th century and now into this century that have suffered more than the Ukrainian people, between World War I, World War II, the Soviet occupation, and now these horrible things. Let's hope that we can try to find a peaceful answer and get the Russians out of their country and return to some sort of democratic rule and rule of law.

Just one or two other thoughts, and that is the shell companies, this was a very good tipoff today, that to solve the problem we have got to make sure that you can't have companies that nobody knows who runs the companies begin to control and own assets. We need to know who controls various assets and various amounts of wealth in a society. Shell companies are something I was not aware of being a problem. Thank you very much for that tipoff today.

Also, again, I think that we need to make sure that we examine our own banking system and financial system here so that it does not encourage corrupt practices in other countries. We have given foreign aid to countries in Africa, for example, where the African dictator ends up being overthrown, and then we find out all the money that we gave has gone overseas to some European or otherwise bank.

And then, of course, by the way, the banks don't ever give the money up. What do the banks do with the money once some petty dictator gangster in the Third World has given them $1 billion in deposits? What do they do with it? They envelop it into their own system. They are the ones who end up with the loot.

Well, there will be future hearings on this issue, and we need to work on that before we start pointing fingers at everybody else right now, because we have some things we can do to help the situation become better.

So with that said, I really have enjoyed this hearing. I hope you did too.

And thank you, Mr. Meeks. I think we have had a very good discussion.

And until next year, then, this committee is adjourned.

[Whereupon, at 12:02 p.m., the subcommittee was adjourned.]

APPENDIX

MATERIAL SUBMITTED FOR THE RECORD

SUBCOMMITTEE HEARING NOTICE
COMMITTEE ON FOREIGN AFFAIRS
U.S. HOUSE OF REPRESENTATIVES
WASHINGTON, DC 20515-6128

**Subcommittee on Europe, Eurasia, and Emerging Threats, Dana Rohrabacher (R-CA),
Chairman**

December 2, 2016

TO: MEMBERS OF THE COMMITTEE ON FOREIGN AFFAIRS

You are respectfully requested to attend an OPEN hearing of the Committee on Foreign Affairs, to be held by the Subcommittee on Europe, Eurasia, and Emerging Threats in Room 2172 of the Rayburn House Office Building (and available live on the Committee website at http://www.ForeignAffairs.house.gov):

DATE: Wednesday, December 7, 2016

TIME: 10:00 a.m.

SUBJECT: Corruption: A Danger to Democracy in Europe and Eurasia

WITNESSES: Mr. Charles Davidson
                   Executive Director
                   Kleptocracy Initiative
                   Hudson Institute

                   Mr. Ivan Vejvoda
                   Senior Vice President for Programs
                   The German Marshall Fund of the United States

                   Mr. Sergei Kolesnikov
                   (Former Co-Founder of Petromed Holding)

By Direction of the Chairman

The Committee on Foreign Affairs seeks to make its facilities accessible to persons with disabilities. If you are in need of special accommodations, please call 202/225-5021 at least four business days in advance of the event, whenever practicable. Questions with regard to special accommodations in general (including availability of Committee materials in alternative formats and assistive listening devices) may be directed to the Committee.

COMMITTEE ON FOREIGN AFFAIRS

MINUTES OF SUBCOMMITTEE ON _____*Europe, Eurasia, and Emerging Threats*_____ HEARING

Day__*Wednesday*__ Date_____*December 7*_____ Room__*2172 Rayburn HOB*__

Starting Time ___*10:05 am*___ Ending Time __*12:02 pm*__

Recesses | *0* | (___to___) (___to___) (___to___) (___to___) (___to___) (___to___)

Presiding Member(s)

Rep. Rohrabacher

Check all of the following that apply:

Open Session ✓   Electronically Recorded (taped) ✓
Executive (closed) Session ☐   Stenographic Record ✓
Televised ☐

TITLE OF HEARING:

Corruption: A Danger to Democracy in Europe and Eurasia

SUBCOMMITTEE MEMBERS PRESENT:

Rep. Meeks, Rep. Weber, Rep. Gabbard

NON-SUBCOMMITTEE MEMBERS PRESENT: *(Mark with an * if they are not members of full committee.)*

Rep. Connolly

HEARING WITNESSES: Same as meeting notice attached? Yes ✓ No ☐
(If "no", please list below and include title, agency, department, or organization.)

STATEMENTS FOR THE RECORD: *(List any statements submitted for the record.)*

Attached Statement from Rep. Connolly

TIME SCHEDULED TO RECONVENE _____
or
TIME ADJOURNED ___*12:02 pm*___

Subcommittee Staff Associate

Statement for the Record
Submitted by Mr. Connolly of Virginia

This Committee must examine three distinct concerns regarding corruption in Europe and Eurasia and how efforts to combat these threats are integral to protecting U.S. national security. The first and greatest threat is Russia's concerted, state-directed effort to buy influence and erode the rule of law in countries on its periphery and beyond. The second is the challenge posed by corruption to democratization in our existing and emerging partners in the region. The final concern is that a creeping problem with conflict of interest in the next U.S. administration develops into a full-fledged threat to the foreign policy priorities of the United States.

As the Center for Strategic and International Studies has noted, "Russia has cultivated an opaque web of economic and political patronage across the region that the Kremlin uses to influence and direct decisionmaking." In Russia, corruption is sui generis. Russia exploits state resources to intervene in the internal affairs of other European countries and gain influence in obscure ways. Through a combination of espionage and dark money, Russia has been financing far-right parties in the United Kingdom, France, Germany, Greece, Bulgaria, Hungary, and elsewhere. These parties generally oppose giving more power to the European Union and favor closer relations with Russia. This strategy seeks to erode confidence in democratic standards and sow seeds of doubt planted by the global financial crisis. Such deliberate efforts to influence the domestic politics of other sovereign countries, while simultaneously undermining Western-style democratic systems, promote instability and threaten national security.

There is also the type of corruption that the United States is actively engaged in rooting out through regional partnerships and our support of democratization processes in Central and Eastern Europe. Funding for anti-corruption assistance through the U.S. Department of State and the U.S. Agency for International Development has steadily risen from $49.5 million in FY 2012 to $118.9 million in FY 2015. In countries like Ukraine, where the U.S. Government has helped to establish a new national anti-corruption bureau, the U.S. has prioritized anti-corruption efforts to enhance people's faith in government and Western-style democracy.

It has become abundantly clear by now that President-elect Donald Trump's sprawling business empire creates expansive conflicts of interest that could lead to accusations of corruption if not adequately addressed. In order to avoid embroiling his incoming administration in a multifaceted corruption scandal, it is imperative that Mr. Trump take immediate steps to place his business ventures in a real blind trust. Otherwise, how can we protect ourselves from the inevitable conflict between Trump's business interests and broader national interests of the American people?

According to the U.S. Department of State's 2015 Quadrennial Diplomacy and Development Review, the estimated total cost of corruption could end world hunger, achieve universal mobile broadband connectivity by 2030, and close the gap between infrastructure needs and available public funds worldwide, and still have two trillion dollars in reserve.

However, the cost of corruption is not limited to foregone investments sacrificed to graft and bribery. Corruption undermines people's fundamental faith in government and society. This is the greater threat we must combat. I look forward to a discussion about how the United States can counter Russian efforts to promote disillusionment with governments it opposes, help our partners and allies root out domestic corruption, and lead by example in eliminating the conflict of interest that allows corruption to flourish.